YORK NOTES

LYRICAL BALLADS

WILLIAM WORDSWORTH AND SAMUEL TAYLOR COLERIDGE

NOTES BY STEVE EDDY

Longman

 York Press

The right of Steve Eddy to be identified as Author of
this Work has been asserted by him in accordance
with the Copyright, Designs and Patents Act 1988

YORK PRESS
322 Old Brompton Road, London SW5 9JH

PEARSON EDUCATION LIMITED
Edinburgh Gate, Harlow,
Essex CM20 2JE, United Kingdom
Associated companies, branches and representatives throughout the world

First published 2009

10 9 8 7 6 5 4 3 2 1

ISBN 978–1–4082–1732–0

Phototypeset by Carnegie Publishing
Printed in China

Contents

PART THREE
CRITICAL APPROACHES

PART FOUR
CRITICAL PERSPECTIVES

PART FIVE
BACKGROUND

PART ONE

INTRODUCTION

STUDYING POEMS

Reading poems and exploring them critically can be approached in a number of ways, but when reading a poem for the first time it is a good idea to consider some, or all, of the following:

- **Format and style**: how do poems differ from other types of text? Does the poem capture a single moment in time, tell a whole story, or make a specific point?

- **The poet's perspective**: consider what the poet has to say, how he or she presents a particular view of people, the world, society, ideas, issues, etc. Are, or were, these views controversial?

- **Verse and metre**: how are **stanzas** or patterns of lines used to reveal the **narrative**? What rhythms and rhymes does the poet use to convey an atmosphere or achieve an effect?

- **Choice of language**: does the poet choose to write formally or informally? Does he or she use different registers for different voices in the poem, vary the sound and style, employ literary techniques such as **imagery**, **alliteration** and **metaphor**?

- **Links and connections**: what other texts does this poem remind you of? Can you see connections between its narrative, main characters and ideas and those of other texts you have studied? Is the poem part of a tradition or literary movement?

- **Your perspective and that of others**: what are your feelings about the poem? Can you relate to its emotions, themes and ideas? What do others say about the poem – for example, critics or other poets and writers?

These York Notes offer an introduction to *Lyrical Ballads* and cannot substitute for close reading of the text and the study of secondary sources.

 **CHECK THE BOOK**
Andrew Keanie's *The Student Guide to William Wordsworth* (Greenwich Exchange, 2000) is a good place to start. It explores Wordsworth's politics, philosophy of poetry, and relationships. Keanie has also written a guide to Coleridge (Greenwich Exchange, 2002).

READING LYRICAL BALLADS

READING LYRICAL BALLADS

CONTEXT

The Augustans took their name from the fact that the classical poets who influenced them were alive during the reign of the Roman Emperor Augustus Caesar (63BCE–19CE).

When Wordsworth and Coleridge published the first edition of *Lyrical Ballads* in 1798 it was a major literary event – though few people realised it at the time. As one twentieth-century reviewer wrote, the collection 'must have come on like punk rock to a public groaning under the weight of over-cooked Augustanisms' (*Guardian*, 29 May 1999). The Augustan poets referred to here had dominated eighteenth-century poetry. They included men like Alexander Pope (1688–1744), James Thomson (1700–48), Thomas Gray (1716–71), and Oliver Goldsmith (?1730–74). Their poetry focuses on the intellect rather than the emotions, is strongly influenced by classical poets such as Virgil, Horace and Ovid, and employs a formal and self-consciously 'poetic' **diction**. Moreover it assumes that the subject matter of poetry should be conventionally elevated, refined, and aimed at a predominantly aristocratic or privileged audience.

CONTEXT

Alexander Pope, the leading eighteenth-century Augustan poet, is most famous for *The Rape of the Lock*, a **satirical** mock-heroic **narrative** poem. A classicist, he is also known for his translation of Homer's *Iliad*.

Wordsworth and Coleridge, though both only in their twenties, were the leading pioneers of the **Romantic** Movement, and in their remarkable poetic collaboration they challenged all the assumptions of the Augustans. They felt that the elitist subject matter and 'poetic' diction of the Augustan poets should be swept aside by poems about ordinary people experiencing the passions, joys and suffering common to all humanity, written in 'a selection of language really used by men', as Wordsworth wrote in his Preface to the 1802 edition.

Wordsworth and Coleridge met and became friends in Bristol in 1795, where Wordsworth may have attended Coleridge's lectures. They became admirers of each other's poetry, spent much of their time together – along with Dorothy Wordsworth – and began a number of collaborative projects. *Lyrical Ballads* is the only one that came to fruition, but it is a remarkable achievement. Although the two poets are different in many ways, they managed to agree on a radical set of poetic aims which are embodied in *Lyrical Ballads* and explained in Wordsworth's 1802 Preface. It is helpful – if not essential – to bear these aims in mind when reading the poems, in order to appreciate them fully. At the heart of their approach was a belief that poetry should enlighten its readers, making them more compassionate, more moral, and more appreciative of the beauty in the world. Equally important, though, was for it to do this by giving pleasure, even while dealing with painful subjects – which they felt were made more bearable by the natural enjoyment afforded by a skilled and varied use of **metre**. Wordsworth, especially, also insisted on the importance of thought in poetry: it is important to realise that he and Coleridge were not simply rejecting Augustan intellect in favour of an outpouring of Romantic feeling. True, they valued personal feeling, but they believed that it was necessary for the poet to reflect on his feelings and their significance, and to draw conclusions. Wordsworth wrote in the Preface that each poem in *Lyrical Ballads* had 'a worthy *purpose*', and that to express this required thought:

> … all good Poetry is the spontaneous overflow of powerful feelings; but though this be true, Poems to which any value can be attached were never produced on any variety of subjects but by a man who, being possessed of more than usual organic sensibility, had also thought long and deeply.

To appreciate *Lyrical Ballads*, therefore, it is necessary to be aware of the interplay of feelings and ideas in the poems. Of course, the subjects which excite the poets' feelings and exercise their intellects are not those of the Augustans. The Augustans only ever wrote about the poor in an idealised form in pastoral poetry, but the poems in *Lyrical Ballads* frequently feature individuals who are poor and oppressed. Thus a major theme of the collection is the collective inhumanity of society – or, to quote 'Lines written in Early Spring', 'what man has made of man' (24). Such poems as 'The Female Vagrant', 'Simon Lee, the Old Huntsman' and 'The Mad Mother' are unflinching portrayals of individuals in situations of great deprivation and hardship. 'The Dungeon', by Coleridge, and 'The Convict', by Wordsworth, also make extreme calls on our sympathy, but with a more obvious argument for social reform.

This concern with the neglected or downtrodden individual extends in *The Rime of the Ancyent Marinere* to a broader exploration of the individual's relationship with society, its subject being a man

CONTEXT

Many critics regard Wordsworth's younger sister Dorothy as a major influence on his poetry. A description of daffodils in her journal, for example, quite closely resembles the one made famous in Wordsworth's poem 'Daffodils'.

CONTEXT

A later **Romantic** poet who was perhaps more sensual and emotional in his approach to poetry was John Keats (1795–1821).

who, because of his crime against nature, has incurred a supernatural punishment in the form of ostracisation by his fellow men. The subject of 'Lines left upon a Seat in a Yew-tree' has distanced himself from society by his own pride. The unfortunate **narrator** of 'The Complaint of a Forsaken Indian Woman', on the other hand, has been abandoned by her tribe because she is too ill to travel with them. She stoically awaits death, at the same time grieving the loss of her child. This poem, in fact, combines two major themes of the collection: death and motherhood. The latter is identified by Wordsworth as such in his Preface, and is explored in several of the poems, especially in 'The Thorn' and 'The Idiot Boy'. 'The Idiot Boy', in common with 'We Are Seven' and 'Anecdote for Fathers', also explores a theme which is a counterpoint to that of man's inhumanity, namely that of childhood innocence.

While many of the poems relate to death and deprivation, others express a great sense of joy. This may be in a mother's powerful love for her child, as in 'The Idiot Boy', or the poet's deep love of nature, as in 'The Nightingale, a Conversational Poem', 'Expostulation and Reply', 'The Tables Turned; an Evening Scene, on the same subject', 'Lines written at a small distance from my House' and, most memorably, 'Lines written a few miles above Tintern Abbey'. Although the first of these is by Coleridge, it is Wordsworth who is the supreme poet of nature. However, one should not read his nature poems expecting a close examination of the details of nature as found in the poems of John Clare (1793–1864) or Anne Brontë (1820–49). Rather, Wordsworth's poems move from a broad picture of nature to a **pantheistic** contemplation of the spirit that moves throughout nature, and of nature's beneficial effect on the human mind.

It was a natural extension of the two poets' wish to portray ordinary people, rather than the wealthy and educated classes, that they chose to incorporate into the collection many aspects of the **ballad** form, the ballad being a traditional **narrative** poem created by, and aimed at, ordinary people. Ballads were often sung rather than read, so they were accessible to the illiterate. This choice was therefore controversial, and very non-Augustan. Indeed, calling the collection *Lyrical Ballads* was itself something of a challenge to the reading public, as well as being almost a contradiction in terms.

CONTEXT

Although Wordsworth, rather than Coleridge, is regarded as the great nature poet of the pair, 'The Nightingale, a Conversational Poem' by Coleridge includes close observation of the actual song of the nightingale. None of Wordsworth's nature poems focus so closely on the detail of nature.

Although only *The Rime of the Ancyent Marinere* is in strictly traditional ballad form, many of the poems are, loosely speaking, ballads in that they tell a story, and do so in rhyming **stanzas**. The power of narrative is referred to in *The Rime of the Ancyent Marinere*, where we see the wedding guest reduced to a childlike state by the Ancient Mariner's tale. This was no doubt one reason for Wordsworth and Coleridge choosing this form. However, as modern readers we should bear in mind several factors. First, we may now find certain aspects of the ballad style off-putting, such as the occasionally chiming rhymes and the deliberate use of repetition, as in 'Goody Blake and Harry Gill':

> Oh! what's the matter? what's the matter?
> What is't ails young Harry Gill?
> That evermore his teeth they chatter,
> Chatter, chatter, chatter still. (1–4)

In addition, we may want to know why we are being told the story, especially in the light of Wordsworth's assertion that every poem in *Lyrical Ballads* has 'a worthy purpose'. *The Rime of the Ancyent Marinere* is a highly engaging tale, but it is also an **allegorical** exploration of the psyche, as well as a study of the individual's relation to society, and of nature and the supernatural. Other narrative poems in the collection have a moral purpose, for example 'The Thorn' and 'The Female Vagrant', though the moral lesson is often learned by the poem's narrator, as in 'Anecdote for Fathers', so that there is no sense of the poet adopting a stance of moral superiority to the reader. As narratives, the poems vary in the degree of satisfaction they afford. On completing *The Rime of the Ancyent Marinere* one has a strong sense of a proper resolution. The Ancient Mariner has achieved a degree of redemption, even if condemned to tell and retell his tale for the rest of his life. 'The Last of the Flock', however, offers no such sense of resolution, while 'The Female Vagrant' not only offers no resolution, but concludes with its narrator ending her tale and weeping 'because she had no more to say/ Of that perpetual weight which on her spirit lay' (270). Some readers will find such endings unsatisfactory, while on reading 'Old Man Travelling', they may wonder what was the point of telling this fragmentary and seemingly inconsequential tale at all.

 CHECK THE POEM
Many of John Clare's poems rejoice in descriptions of nature. See for example 'The Badger', in John Clare, *Collected Poems* (OUP).

 CHECK THE POEM
One classic traditional **ballad** is the anonymous 'Ballad of Sir Patrick Spens', widely available online. It tells the story of an ill-fated sea voyage made on the order of a king of Scotland. A Victorian ballad featuring a doomed sea voyage is 'Lord Franklin', which is about the real expedition of Lord Franklin to find the North-West Passage around the Pole.

CHECK THE BOOK

The term 'unreliable narrator' was coined by Wayne C. Booth (1921–2005) in his classic study in literary criticism *The Rhetoric of Fiction* (Chicago University Press, 1983).

CHECK THE BOOK

The use of the 'unreliable narrator' and the 'partial narrative' was very new when *Lyrical Ballads* was published. One of the earliest occurrences is Emily Brontë's *Wuthering Heights* (1847), whose Nellie Dean is biased in her narrative, while Lockwood, the other main narrator, is a poor judge of character. There are also tantalising gaps in the narrative, comparable with that in 'The Idiot Boy'. For example, we never know where Heathcliff disappears to for several years.

At other times the reader has to take into account that the narrative poems may have 'unreliable' or partially informed narrators. It is always important to remember that, even when a poem is written in the first person, we cannot assume that the poet is simply speaking in his own voice and expressing his own views. The rather gossipy narrator of 'The Thorn', for example, is definitely not Wordsworth himself. Nor can he do more than relay what he knows of the woman's story and speculate on local gossip: we never know whether or not she killed her baby – or even if she had one. 'The Idiot Boy' is also a partial narrative, because its main character, Johnny, is incapable of relating the details of his moonlight journey in an intelligible way. Even here, moreover, although Wordsworth rather strains credulity by imploring the muses to reveal these details, and complaining that they have been denied him, we cannot quite assume that the narrator is simply Wordsworth himself.

The feature that most challenged Wordsworth's contemporaries, however, is one that continues to baffle many modern readers: namely, the fact that much of the language, in attempting to echo that spoken by ordinary lower-class people, frequently borders on the simplistic. For a modern student, this at least means that most of the poems are relatively easy to read, especially with the aid of a glossary to explain those words which have dropped out of usage or changed in meaning. Grammatical complexity is rare in *Lyrical Ballads*. The disadvantage is that the simplicity of the **diction** may blind the reader to the depths of meaning. 'The Thorn', for example, the poem identified by Wordsworth as being the most plain in language, is often criticised for its triteness, and especially for one **stanza:**

This thorn you on your left espy;
And to the left, three yards beyond,
You see a little muddy pond
Of water, never dry;
I've measured it from side to side:
'Tis three feet long, and two feet wide. (30–5)

No one could fail to understand the sense of these lines. However, the poem contains **symbolism** that can easily be overlooked, and even the prosaic use of measurements can at least be partly justified by the narrator's wish to impress on us that this is a real story, with a real setting that he has visited himself. The concrete, verifiable nature of these details is in contrast to the mystery surrounding the poem's main character, Martha Ray.

Fortunately the lines quoted above are an extreme case. Most of the poems combine energy with a freshness and sincerity of diction. At times, too, there is striking **imagery**, especially in *The Rime of the Ancyent Marinere*. Often, as in 'Lines written a few miles above Tintern Abbey', there is deep reflection on nature and the human spirit, expressed with an eloquence that never strays into unnecessary complication.

One remaining question is that of how far *Lyrical Ballads* can be regarded as a whole. The longest poem in the collection, *The Rime of the Ancyent Marinere*, was jointly conceived by Coleridge and Wordsworth, though largely written by Coleridge alone. However, only three other poems are by Coleridge: 'The Foster-Mother's Tale', 'The Nightingale, a Conversational Poem' and 'The Dungeon'. Added to this, Wordsworth later came to feel that *The Rime of the Ancyent Marinere* harmed the collection, partly because it came first, and its occasionally archaic language, used in imitation of old ballads, had the effect of deterring some readers from continuing. Increasingly, too, Wordsworth took over the collection, adding many poems to subsequent editions and making major amendments to others. Some editors therefore regard *Lyrical Ballads* as an ongoing project consisting of several editions, in which Wordsworth was increasingly prominent. The first edition, however (the one referred to in these Notes), has the virtue of representing the collaboration in the form in which it made its first shockingly radical appearance on the British poetry scene.

CONTEXT

Wordsworth himself did not continue to regard the poems in *Lyrical Ballads* as necessarily parts of a whole. 'Lines written a few miles above Tintern Abbey', which is definitely not a **ballad**, was included largely because he finished it just as the book was being printed and there was just enough time to include it before the book was published. He later split up the poems across a number of publications.

CONTEXT

In addition to moving *The Rime of the Ancyent Marinere* further into the book, in later editions Wordsworth also had Coleridge's name removed from the cover.

PART TWO

THE TEXT

NOTE ON THE TEXT

Lyrical Ballads was first published anonymously, by Joseph Cottle, in 1798. It was then republished by Longmans in 1800, and again in 1802. The poems in the Penguin Classics edition, ed. Michael Schmidt (1999, reprinted 2006), which has been used in these Notes, are as published in the original Cottle edition. The Preface occasionally referred to is Wordsworth's from the 1802 edition, which can be found in *Lyrical Ballads* (second edition, ed. Michael Mason, Pearson, 2007).

DETAILED SUMMARIES

CONTEXT

The central incident of the poem – the killing of the albatross – is based on Captain George Shelvocke's *Voyage Round the World by Way of the Great South Sea* (1726). Shelvocke describes how his second mate shot a black albatross while they were rounding Cape Horn. In the 1840s Wordsworth told a friend that it was he, not Coleridge, who had been reading this book.

THE RIME OF THE ANCYENT MARINERE

This is Coleridge's most important contribution to *Lyrical Ballads*, and the longest poem in the collection. However, the poem was originally conceived jointly by Wordsworth and Coleridge. The two poets intended to write it together, but this proved to be too difficult. Wordsworth reportedly later told his friend the Reverend Alexander Dyce in the 1840s: 'I had very little share in the composition of it, for I soon found that the style of Coleridge and myself would not assimilate.' Wordsworth claimed to have written the lines 'And thou art long and lank, and brown,/ As is the ribbed Sea-sand' (220–1) as well as the fifth **stanza** of Part I and 'four or five more in different parts of the poem'. He added: 'The idea of shooting an albatross was mine ... I also suggested the reanimation of the dead bodies, to work the ship' (quoted in D. and S. Coleridge (eds.) *The Poems of Samuel Taylor Coleridge*, 1852).

More than any other poem in the collection, *The Rime of the Ancyent Marinere* is composed in deliberate imitation of the traditional **ballad** form. It is notionally set in the late fifteenth or early sixteenth century, between the voyages of Columbus (1492) and Magellan (1519), a great period of discovery, and the use of archaic words and spellings such as 'countree' and 'drouth' reflects this. Many of these were modernised in later editions of *Lyrical Ballads*, partly in response to criticism. The verse form reflects Coleridge's attempt to imitate a traditional ballad: it is in largely **iambic quatrains** made up of alternate unrhymed and rhymed lines, the unrhymed lines having four stresses and the rhymed ones three. This form is found in many traditional ballads. Coleridge's practice of adding occasional extra lines, as in Part II, stanza 4, also echoes some traditional ballads. However, his use of internal rhymes (usually in the third line of the quatrain), as in Part I, stanza 15, is his own innovation.

The poem is a **framed narrative**, set in the context of a wedding, at which the mysterious mariner exercises a seemingly supernatural power to compel one of the wedding guests to hear his story. However, although the mariner has this power, he is himself compelled to tell and retell his tale, as if only by doing so can he gain temporary relief from the post-traumatic anguish of his experience. In this respect he resembles the Wandering Jew. This compulsion can also be seen as an extension of the curse he brings upon himself by killing the albatross. The wedding context is significant in that a wedding represents social harmony and the joy of companionship: the blessings from which the mariner has been excluded – at least until being absolved of his sins by the holy man in the final section of the poem. The theme of the individual's alienation from society is central to the poem.

> **CONTEXT**
>
> The legend of the Wandering Jew is part of medieval Christian folklore. He is said to have taunted Jesus as he carried the cross to the site of the Crucifixion. Jesus supposedly condemned him to walk the earth, unable to die, until the Second Coming.

PART I

- The Ancient Mariner forces a guest at a wedding to hear his story.
- He describes sailing to the Antarctic, and then northwards, visited by a wandering albatross.
- He confesses to having shot the bird.

CONTEXT

During the early years of its published life, *The Rime of the Ancyent Marinere* was popular with sea captains, partly because of its careful attention to maritime detail.

CHECK THE BOOK

Most of Shakespeare's comedies end with weddings or wedding plans, because marriage was seen as a symbol of social harmony, as well as actually helping to preserve it by bringing families together. A typical example is *A Midsummer Night's Dream*.

The Ancient Mariner stops a wedding guest, who resists at first, then feels compelled to listen. The old man begins his story, describing how his ship left port and headed south into the Atlantic, then reached the Equator. The bride enters the hall, but the wedding guest still cannot tear himself away. The mariner describes his ship sailing on south into Antarctic waters. An albatross appears out of the fog and the mariners feed it. A southerly wind then springs up, blowing the ship northwards, back towards the Equator. The old man confesses to having shot the albatross.

COMMENTARY

This opening section establishes the **narrative** context of the poem. The mariner is an unexpected and unwelcome visitor at a wedding. His 'glittering eye' (3) immediately suggests something supernatural or at least unusual about him, while his beard shows his age. The fact that he singles out 'one of three' (2) suggests that this guest has a special need to hear the tale and learn from it. Despite this, he at first tries to dismiss the mariner, inviting him to tell his tale to the assembled wedding guests, then threatening him with his staff. The repetition of 'glittering eye' (16), referring to the mariner, reinforces the suggestion that he has a supernatural power that reduces the wedding guest to a childlike state.

The mariner launches straight into his story, beginning with the ship setting sail. Neither ship nor port are named, in keeping with Coleridge's avoidance of all proper nouns in the poem, and the mariner himself remains anonymous. This gives the poem a universality but also a mysterious dreamlike quality. This is added to by Coleridge's method of tracking the voyage, which avoids precise geography. However, since the sun rises 'upon the left' and goes down 'on the right' (29–30) we know that the ship is initially heading south.

The wedding guest at this stage is aware of the wedding proceeding, which causes him to 'beat his breast' because he wants to join the other guests but cannot. His helplessness is echoed by that of the mariners, who are driven 'Like Chaff' (48) by the wind. We are thrown, with the mariners, into a strange and fearsome world of ice which makes threatening animalistic noises (59–60). The mariners are understandably comforted by the albatross, greeting it as if it is a 'Christian Soul' (63). Its arrival seems to help the ship to break through the polar ice.

The bird visits 'for vespers nine' (74), meaning nine evenings, but with the added connotations of vespers meaning evening prayer. Coleridge allows the wedding guest one more line in order to draw attention to the mariner's look of torment. The old man's simple confession is a dramatically arresting end to Part I.

CONTEXT

The phrase 'Christian Soul' applied to the albatross hints at the ancient perception of the soul as a bird, and at the folk belief that some seabirds were the souls of dead sailors in corporeal form.

QUESTION

No explanation is given for the Ancient Mariner killing the albatross. Do you think there is a reason? Is Coleridge's failure to give an explanation a fault, in your view, or does it make the poem stronger by adding to the mystery?

GLOSSARY

48	**Chaff** the unwanted outer husks of ears of wheat – suggesting that the mariners are being rejected
55	**ken** knew, recognised
60	**noises of a swound** such noises as one might dimly hear or imagine when swooning
72	**hollo** call

PART II

- As the ship heads north, the mariners blame the Ancient Mariner for killing the albatross, then change their minds when the fog and mist clear.
- The ship is suddenly becalmed and the mariners again blame the Ancient Mariner, hanging the bird around his neck.

Having traversed the South Pole, the ship is now heading north. The mariners now find that the sun rises on their right – where the east now lies in relation to their position on the globe. They complain that the Ancient Mariner has shot the bird that brought the southerly wind, but then change their minds when the wind picks up after its death, saying instead that it brought 'fog and mist' (96) and that he was right to kill it. As the ship reaches the Equator again it is becalmed and the crew run out of water. There are unnatural portents – 'slimy things' (121) and a coloured fire on the sea. The mariners dream of the 'Spirit' (128) plaguing them. They are dying of thirst and now blame the Ancient Mariner again, punishing him by tying the dead albatross around his neck.

 QUESTION

The phrase 'like God's own head' (93) is changed to 'like an angel's head' in later editions. Do you think this is an improvement?

CONTEXT

The phrase 'copper sky' (107) may stem from the Bible: 'And thy heaven that is over thy head shall be brass, and the earth that is under thee shall be iron' (*King James Authorised Version*, Deuteronomy 28:23).

COMMENTARY

Part II sees the mariners vacillating in their judgement of the Ancient Mariner. First they say he has done 'an hellish thing' (89) in killing the albatross; then, when the sun rises brightly 'like God's own head' (93) rather than being bedimmed, they decide that the bird had been responsible for the fog. The **alliteration** and internal rhymes of the fifth **stanza**, coupled with the image of the mariners bursting into a 'silent Sea' (102), create a mood of freedom and excitement, albeit with a hint of eeriness. However, the mood rapidly changes for the worse in the remaining stanzas, as the wind drops and the ship is becalmed. The image of the sails dropping fits the drooping spirits of the men.

Coleridge's extreme compression of the voyage can be seen. The mariners broke through the South Pole at the end of Part I, and by stanza 7 of Part II they have already reached the Equator again, as shown by the sun standing directly overhead at noon. The 'hot and copper sky' (107) is threatening in its unnaturalness. This sense is heightened by Coleridge's brilliant image of 'a painted Ship/ Upon a painted Ocean' (112–13) (as in a landscape painting). The tedious lack of progress is also made more palpable by the use of repetition in stanzas 8–10, especially in the much-quoted 'Water, water, every where' (115, 117). The image of 'slimy things … with legs' crawling 'Upon the slimy Sea' (121–2) adds to the horror. The 'death-fires' (124) may refer to St Elmo's Fire, a naturally occurring electrostatic phenomenon, and the colourfully burning sea to natural phosphorescence, but the imaginative effects are powerfully supernatural.

An explanation of the supernatural signs is suggested in the mariners' dreams: they are being plagued by a polar spirit, a demon that follows them beneath the sea. Coleridge's images of the thirst that renders the mariners dumb are simple, as befits the **ballad** style, but vividly effective, especially 'choked with soot' (134). Part II ends, like Part I, on a highly dramatic note. Attempting to blame their plight on the Ancient Mariner, the other mariners remove his cross – thus depriving him of its protection, replacing it with the dead albatross.

CONTEXT

Travel writers had described the sea in equatorial regions as seeming to rot, and scientific writers had explained the phenomenon of phosphorescence as being caused by this rotting. Thus Coleridge's **imagery** is based on his research rather than mere fancy.

 QUESTION

The supernatural is seen as a powerful force in *The Rime of the Ancyent Marinere*. At the same time there is Christian significance in the mariners removing the Ancient Mariner's cross. Which of the two forces do you think is the more dominant in the poem?

GLOSSARY

83	**weft** collectively, the horizontal threads in a piece of fabric
124	**Death-fires** possibly St Elmo's Fire (see above), which caused flickering flames or lights on ships' rigging, superstitiously thought to be the souls of the drowned

PART III

- A ghost ship appears and passes by.
- The mariners curse the Ancient Mariner and die.

Seeing a ship in the distance, the Ancient Mariner bites his own arm and sucks his blood to moisten his mouth, and cries 'A sail! A sail!' (153). As the strange ship passes between the mariners and the sun, they see that it is crewed by a ghostly woman and a skeletal man, playing dice. The woman wins and the ghost ship quickly sails away. The moon rises, with a star close by – a bad omen. The mariners curse the Ancient Mariner, then die.

COMMENTARY

In this strange section of the poem the Ancient Mariner spies a ghostly ship which anticipates the fate of his colleagues. The incident is drawn out by the gradual expansion of the ship from a speck on the horizon to a full-sized hulk of a ship that draws alongside the mariners. This is the first time in the voyage that the mariners have encountered another ship. In their desperate plight, they are overjoyed, and the Ancient Mariner is moved to shed his own blood to moisten his mouth in order to cry 'A sail!' (153). However, their joy is short-lived. We see, as they must, that the movement of the approaching ship is unnatural: it has no need to 'tack from side to side' (159) (making indirect progress by use of a side-wind); rather, it sails without the aid of wind or tide, indicating its spectral nature.

The appearance of the ship at evening, when the sea is 'all a flame' with the setting sun (163) suggests death and even hellfire. It seems a worse omen when the ghost ship drives suddenly between the sun and the mariners' ship, giving the impression that the sun is peering through prison bars (171–2). Seeing the gossamer-thin sails and unboarded ribs of the ship, the Ancient Mariner is incredulous: 'Are those *her* Sails .../ Are these *her* naked ribs ...?' (175–8). A woman and her skeletal partner make up the ship's only crew, a hideous and terrifying sight. The ship's bare ribs anticipate those of the skeletal figure. The obvious interpretation of this apparition is that the male

CONTEXT

Coleridge later explained the mariners' grinning (158): 'I took the thought of *grinning for joy* ... from my companion's remark to me, when we had climbed to the top of Plinlimmon, and were nearly dead with thirst. We could not speak from the constriction, till we found a little puddle under a stone. He said to me, "You grinned like an idiot!"'

figure represents Death, while the female represents Sin. Her red lips and 'free' looks (186) suggest unrestrained sexuality, and her leprous skin would have been associated both with venereal disease and moral corruption. However, a gloss added by Coleridge to the 1817 edition of *Lyrical Ballads* states that the skeletal male figure is Death and the woman Life-in-Death, and that she wins the soul of the Ancient Mariner. She seems to represent a cursed state which is neither real life nor real death: the latter would at least offer a sense of resolution, and perhaps redemption.

The woman whistles to call up a wind, and the spectral ship 'darts' (200) away, the word giving an impression of unnaturally quick movement. The crescent moon with a star between its horns (203) is traditionally seen by mariners as a bad omen, which is the immediate reason for the crew silently cursing the Ancient Mariner with their dying gaze. Part III, like the preceding parts, ends dramatically with the death of the mariners, the passing of their souls made vivid by Coleridge's image: 'Like the whiz of my Cross-bow' (214). This links their deaths directly to the Ancient Mariner's killing of the albatross.

CONTEXT

The Reverend Alexander Dyce, a friend of Wordsworth, quoted Wordsworth as having told him, in 1840, 'The Ancient Mariner* was founded on a strange dream, which a friend of Coleridge had, who fancied he saw a skeleton ship, with figures in it.'

GLOSSARY

146	**wist** thought, perceived
147	**water-sprite** a minor water demon
149	**unslack'd** (rhymes with 'bak'd', or baked) unslaked; the men's throats are so dry that they cannot speak
150	**drouth** drought
156	**Gramercy** an expression of astonished gratitude, from the French *grand merci* (great thanks)
160	**work us weal** do us good
161	**steddies** steadies
180	**Pheere** mate (the archaic word was changed to 'mate') in later editions, and could be taken to mean both husband and second in command after a ship's captain
184	**charnel** repository for corpses
195	**sterte** started
201	**clombe above the Eastern bar** climbed above the eastern horizon
207	**ee** eye

QUESTION

Do you feel that Coleridge's use of archaic words improves the poem by making it sound more authentic, or do they just make the poem less accessible?

PART IV

- The Ancient Mariner reassures the wedding guest.
- The Ancient Mariner describes the horror of his loneliness.
- He blesses the water snakes and finds that he can pray.
- The albatross falls from his neck.

In this section of the poem, we are again reminded of its **narrative** framework when the wedding guest says that he fears the Ancient Mariner, who assures him that he is not a ghost: 'This body dropt not down' (223). The Ancient Mariner describes the horror of being completely alone on the ocean, surrounded by 'slimy things' (230) and unable either to pray or die. However, his desolation gives way to at least a partial redemption. When he sees water snakes and, without thinking, blesses them, he suddenly finds that he can pray, and the albatross, **symbol** of his sin and alienation, falls from his neck. The climactic nature of this section is reflected in the unusually high number of **stanzas** in which Coleridge adds one or more lines (usually rhyming) to the usual **quatrain**: six out of fifteen.

For a more detailed discussion of Part IV and the glossary for this section, see **Extended commentaries**.

PART V

- The corpses of the mariners work the ship.
- The Ancient Mariner witnesses strange supernatural phenomena.
- The ship, heading north, reaches the Equator.
- The mariner falls into a trance and two spirits discuss his fate.

The Ancient Mariner manages to sleep. When it rains he is able to drink. The wind starts up and he sees the sky 'burst into life' (306). The rain pours down and the ship moves on, propelled not by the wind but by the polar spirit. The dead mariners rise up and work the ship in silence, the Ancient Mariner working alongside the body of his nephew. Heavenly sounds come from the men's mouths, and fly to the sun and back. The Ancient Mariner hears sweet music.

The polar spirit propels the ship onwards. At noon on the Equator it stands still, and then leaps forward, throwing the Ancient Mariner into a swoon. He then hears two voices discussing his crime in killing the albatross. One explains that the spirit loved the bird, while the other speaks of the Ancient Mariner's penance.

COMMENTARY

The opening praise of sleep as being 'Belov'd from pole to pole' (285) perhaps escapes triteness because the Ancient Mariner has almost literally travelled 'from pole to pole'. Coleridge shows an awareness of the relationship between dreams and real external stimuli when he has the Ancient Mariner dream that the buckets are filled with dew, only to wake and find that it is raining. This continues the symbolism of Part IV: both thirst and its relief are conceived in spiritual terms. His lightness of body may be literal from not eating, and symbolic in that he has become less corporeally attached to the physical world. This prepares him for the strange and apocalyptic events of this part of the poem. A great wind springs up, accompanied by shining 'fire-flags' (305). This

---

CONTEXT

There are many precedents for the association of music with spiritual harmony or divinity. Plato writes of the 'Music of the Spheres', medieval angels are frequently depicted playing musical instruments, and Shakespeare uses music to suggest the divine in *The Tempest*.

 CHECK THE BOOK

In the Ancient Mariner's grateful address to sleep, Coleridge may have had in mind Macbeth's words: 'Sleep that knits up the ravelled sleeve of care' (*Macbeth*, Act II, scene 2).

CONTEXT

The 'fire-flags' of line 305 were perhaps inspired by the Leonid meteor shower which Coleridge, Wordsworth and Dorothy Wordsworth witnessed in 1797.

CHECK THE BOOK

It is lightning which galvanises into activity the corpse in Mary Shelley's *Frankenstein* (1818). Both authors may have been influenced by the experiments of Italian physician and scientist Luigi Galvani (1737–98) into causing muscular movements by electricity in the corpses of frogs. (The word *galvanise* is derived from his name.)

gives rise to a dramatic storm, with a river of lightning which falls straight ('with never a jag', 316) from the sky. The 'river' of lightning continues the symbolic connection between water and the quenching of spiritual thirst. The lightning seems to galvanise the dead men into activity, and, zombie-like, they begin to sail the ship. Ghastly though they appear to the Ancient Mariner, it may be significant that he includes himself among the crew in his statement 'We were a ghastly crew' (331): he now identifies with his shipmates. Similarly, it indicates his new sense of social and familial ties when he describes working alongside 'The body of my brother's son' (332).

With the arrival of dawn, the sailors gather together and 'Sweet sounds' (340) rise from their mouths, fly to the sun, and return, the harmony indicating that the corpses are animated by benign spirits, not demons. With the song of the lavrock (skylark) and other birds, coming to the Ancient Mariner mid-ocean, we seem to be in an increasingly visionary realm. The effect is heightened by the miraculous sounds, one minute 'like all instruments', the next 'like a lonely flute' (351–2). Even after the angelic sounds cease, the Ancient Mariner is lulled by the harmonious sounds of nature (357–60).

Coleridge times his dramatic effect well, having the Ancient Mariner break away from this tranquil description to make an urgent demand for the wedding guest's continued attention – which perhaps has the effect of renewing that of the reader at a point when the tension has relaxed somewhat. The Ancient Mariner warns the wedding guest that he will be 'sadder and wiser' the next day (367–8), before resuming his tale, implying that there are further moral lessons for the wedding guest to learn.

The mariners continue to work the ship, though no longer fixing the Ancient Mariner with their accusing stare. It is now made explicit that it is the polar spirit who moves the ship onwards, but as the vessel reaches the Equator, at noon, it stands still, before once again lurching into action and causing the Ancient Mariner to swoon. The **simile** describing the ship's action as 'like a pawing horse let go' (393) suggests that it is impatient to be free. In his swoon the

Ancient Mariner hears two spirit voices discussing him. They explain that his trials have all been caused by his killing of 'the harmless Albatross' (405). The solitary polar spirit loved the bird, and the bird loved the Ancient Mariner – only to be rewarded by a bolt from his cross-bow. Part V does not end as dramatically as previous parts, but it reveals that the Ancient Mariner has not yet completed his penance.

QUESTION

The dialogue between the two spirits is used to explain the ship's windless progress, but it also interrupts the main **narrative**. How well do you think it works dramatically?

GLOSSARY

289	**silly** ordinary
304	**sere** withered
310	**sedge** reeds: the wind in the sails makes a sound like the wind in the reeds
316	**with never a jag** straight rather than jagged
350	**jargoning** birdsong (a Chaucerian word)
374	**n'old** would not
396	**swound** swoon

PART VI

- The spirits discuss the ship's movement and then depart.
- The Ancient Mariner awakes.
- The crew stare at him and he is unable to pray.
- As the ship approaches port, angelic forms stand on the mariners' corpses.
- A boat appears carrying a pilot, his boy and a hermit.

The spirits discuss why the ship is flying on so fast and depart to avoid being 'belated' (431). The Ancient Mariner awakes. The dead stand on the deck and fix stony eyes upon him. Again he cannot pray. But then the spell is broken and he sees the ocean but cannot look back for fear. A new breeze springs up blowing on him alone. The ship approaches the Ancient Mariner's homeland. The dead men lie flat on the deck but an angelic form stands on each corpse waving to the land. A boat appears carrying a pilot, his boy and a hermit.

COMMENTARY

In this penultimate part, there is a general sense of the Ancient Mariner being on the homeward stretch. He has achieved a partial redemption, the dead men's souls are on their way to heaven, and there is renewed hope as the ship approaches land. First, however, the two spirit voices discuss the situation. Notionally, the second is explaining to the first, but this is actually for the reader's benefit. The second spirit explains the mechanics of the ship's movement: the ocean 'hath no blast [wind]' (419) but the air is somehow sucked out, or sliced in two, before the ship, to rejoin behind it, which has the effect of drawing it swiftly onwards. The sea is also **personified** as awaiting the moon's tidal guidance. However, none of this makes clear who or what is responsible for the ship's progress, or why this will slow down when the Ancient Mariner regains consciousness.

On waking, the Ancient Mariner seems to be briefly set back. The dead men are once more staring accusingly at him, and once more he finds he is unable to pray. However, the spell is broken and he can move his eyes. He looks to the north, in the direction in which the ship is moving, but not back. Coleridge explains, evocatively, that the Ancient Mariner is like someone 'on a lonesome road' who cannot look back for fear of 'a frightful fiend' following him (440–4). The word 'tread' subtly conveys the stealthy movement of the imagined fiend.

The wind, the 'meadow-gale of spring' (461), that blows on the Ancient Mariner brings hope of positive change. It blows 'Sweetly, sweetly' (466), a phrase which anticipates the Ancient Mariner's joyfully incredulous sighting of his homeland. It is a powerfully atmospheric moment when the Ancient Mariner sees the shadows of the dead men rising up in the moonlight. Their colouring connects them to the seraphim, the highest order of angels, who were said to glow red with their love of God. They make an arresting picture, with their right arms burning aloft like torches and their eyeballs glittering – as the Ancient Mariner's are said to do

---

CONTEXT

The lines 'His great bright eye most silently/ Up to the moon is cast' (420–1) are paraphrased from the *Orchestra* by the Elizabethan poet Sir John Davies (1569–1626): 'For his great chrystall eye is always cast/ Up to the Moone, and on her fixèd fast.' Poet and critic T. S. Eliot preferred Davies's lines to those of Coleridge.

by the wedding guest. The Ancient Mariner prays and turns his head away. When he looks back he sees an angel of light standing over every corpse, standing 'as signals to the land' (520), representatives of the spiritual realm, offering guidance to humanity. Their silence is like music to the Ancient Mariner, again, as earlier, suggesting divine harmony. The contrast between spiritual and temporal is made by the 'dash of oars' (526) intruding on this silence. The part ends on a note of gathering optimism, as the Ancient Mariner looks forward to being absolved of his sin by the hermit.

CHECK THE BOOK

The Ancient Mariner's inability to pray is like that of Claudius in Shakespeare's *Hamlet* (Act III, scene 3), who cannot pray because he has murdered his brother and does not fully repent the crime, or like Macbeth, who cannot say 'Amen' after murdering Duncan (*Macbeth*, Act II, scene 2). In the case of the Ancient Mariner it is the dead men's curse that shuts him off from divine grace.

GLOSSARY	
431	**belated** caught out after darkness falls
439	**charnel-dungeon** repository for corpses, with the added suggestion of a prison cell
444	**een** eyes
470	**Kirk** church
489	**rood** cross (of the Crucifixion)
516	**seraph-man** angelic man, or angel
526	**Eftsones** all too soon
527	**pilot** someone whose job it is to lead ships into harbour
541	**hermit** holy man who chooses to live alone and in poverty in order to pursue his spiritual practice
544	**shrieve** shrive; hear confession of and absolve from sins

PART VII

- The boat's occupants wonder at the ghastly ship.
- The ship sinks.
- The pilot rescues the Ancient Mariner but then has a fit.
- The Ancient Mariner begs the hermit to take his confession and is compelled to tell his tale.
- The Ancient Mariner tells the wedding guest that it is sweet to go to church, then leaves.

The hermit is described, then the occupants of the boat are amazed by the ghastly ship. The pilot is worried, but the hermit urges him on. There is a rumbling sound beneath the ship, which then sinks. The pilot rescues the Ancient Mariner, but when the Ancient Mariner moves his lips the pilot shrieks. The Ancient Mariner takes the oars and the boy laughs crazily. The Ancient Mariner begs the hermit to hear his confession and absolve him. The hermit asks what kind of man he is and the Ancient Mariner is compelled to tell his tale. To the wedding guest he adds that every so often the agony comes over him again and he is compelled to recount the tale anew.

The sound of loud celebration is now coming from the wedding. The Ancient Mariner tells the wedding guest how alone he has been, but that now it is sweet to go to church in company and pray, adding that love for our fellow man and all God's creatures is a form of prayer. The Ancient Mariner finally goes, leaving the wedding guest 'a sadder and a wiser man' (655).

QUESTION

At the point when the pilot's boat appears, do you expect the Ancient Mariner to be rescued and fully absolved? What signs are there in the text of what is to come, and how are we kept in suspense?

COMMENTARY

Two opening **stanzas** are devoted to the hermit – the first time the **narrative** has departed from ship, sea and sailors. The time frame here is uncertain, but on the whole it seems that the Ancient Mariner knew the hermit before setting sail, or at least knew of him, and therefore has faith in his willingness and ability to help. His loud hymns and liking for mariners bode well for the Ancient Mariner. His 'cushion plump' (552) for a moment suggests self-indulgence, before we learn that this is merely the moss on the oak-stump. This identifies the hermit with nature. However, there is a marked ambiguity in the **imagery** of nature presented by the hermit. He compares the ship's sails to 'skeletons of leaves' (565), recalling the skeletal figure of Death on the ghostly hulk (Part III), and pictures the ivy 'heavy with snow' (567), rather gratuitously adding the image of the cannibalistic wolf. Perhaps Coleridge's intention is to emphasise that the Ancient Mariner and his ship present an unnerving spectacle to the boat's occupants, which, together with their bafflement at the disappearance of the lights they saw on board the ship, makes them more than a little wary.

It is another climactic moment when the ship sinks, accompanied by a 'loud and dreadful sound' (582). Someone saves the Ancient Mariner, but his appearance is clearly frightening: when he speaks, the pilot literally has a fit and the hermit begins to pray, while the pilot's boy, taking the mariner to be the Devil, goes mad (601). Even on dry land the hermit can hardly stand, and anxiously challenges the Ancient Mariner. We are never told whether the hermit actually grants him absolution, but the Ancient Mariner explains that he is still impelled to retell his tale from time to time, so his redemption is clearly only partial. Moreover, he has to travel 'like night, from land to land' (618), the comparison suggesting an enduring darkness in the man, as well as his restlessness. As a form of penance, he has to tell his tale to certain people who presumably have a moral need to hear and heed it. This of course now includes the reader of the poem.

The return to the uproar of the wedding is a sudden contrast which clears the air in anticipation of the end of the poem, when the reader must be removed from the supernatural world and returned to normality. In lines 628–31 the Ancient Mariner sums up for the wedding guest, and us, what his experience has been – essentially one of intense loneliness. Understandably, he now values going to church 'With a goodly company', and being part of an all-inclusive community. His sense of community is one based on universal love for 'man and bird and beast' (644), 'All things both great and small' (646). He has evidently learned the lesson of the albatross. His mystique is preserved by his abrupt disappearance in the

CONTEXT

The hermit's mossy oak-stump also suggests druidry, since the oak was sacred to the druids. This would be consistent with the spirituality of the poem being part-Christian, part-pagan.

What are your views on the wedding guest being left 'A sadder and a wiser man' (655)? What has he learned, and why should this sadden him?

penultimate **stanza** of the poem. His departure is not described; he simply 'Is gone' (651). The wedding guest, too, appears to have learned a lesson, since he is 'A sadder and a wiser man' (655). We are left to ponder on why this message of universal love should leave him a sadder man as well as a wiser one.

GLOSSARY

550	**Contrée** country	
591	**telling of the sound** echoing	
617	**ghastly aventure** appalling adventure, or ordeal	
626	**Vesper-bell** bell for evening prayer	

THE FOSTER-MOTHER'S TALE

CHECK THE POEM

'The Foster-Mother's Tale' resembles, in some ways, a later poem by Emily Brontë, 'The Prisoner', also published as 'A Fragment', because it was originally taken from a longer poem. Both poems are **gothic** in character, and are **framed narratives** telling the story, within a story, of someone unjustly imprisoned in a dungeon.

- A foster-mother denies all knowledge of a man apparently mentioned by the young woman whom she has fostered.
- The young woman says this unknown man has left her troubled – then breaks off to ask about a dungeon entrance.
- The foster-mother explains that her father-in-law made it to enable the escape of an imprisoned youth, last seen sailing up a remote river.

This rather odd dramatic fragment is from Coleridge's tragedy *Osorio*. There is no obvious reason for the fragment to begin where it does, and later editions of *Lyrical Ballads* begin it with the foster-mother's question 'Can no one hear?' (17). The mystery man alluded to at the start of the fragment in the Penguin edition does not appear later in the fragment, and although the foster-mother's description of happy times with her young charges, Maria and Albert, is touching, it is not directly relevant to the story of the wild boy that takes up most of the poem. It was perhaps included originally as it relates to one of the main themes of the collection, as identified by Wordsworth – namely, motherly love. If it does relate in any way to the wild boy's story, it is in that he has known no such motherly love, having been abandoned as a baby. The poem is largely a **gothic** mystery about a child of nature.

COMMENTARY

The foster-mother is very fond of Maria, whom she addresses as 'my sweet lady' (5). This term, and the fact that she recalls the children teaching her what they had learned, and how to speak 'In gentle phrase' (10) reveals that the foster-mother is of a lower social class than Maria and Albert. Maria speaks in an elevated way – not like the homely characters of Wordsworth's poems. Her lengthy and grammatically complex sentence describing how the mystery man has left her troubled with wild fancies has echoes of Shakespeare's nobles, who usually speak in **blank verse**, unlike his commoners, and contradicts the avowed intention of the *Lyrical Ballads* to use only the language of the common man. Indeed the whole poem is in blank verse, as used by Shakespeare for most of his noble characters' lines.

QUESTION

What do you think Coleridge gains, if anything, by beginning the fragment where he does, rather than with the words 'Can no one hear?' (17)?

The foster-mother seems worried that she will be overheard telling Maria the story explaining the entrance to the dungeon, even though the events have long passed. She relates how her father-in-law, Leoni (now dead), found a baby beneath a tree. The way in which the child was wrapped up indicates immediately that this is a child of nature, someone who lacks the socialising and restricting influence of ordinary parentage, and who will probably not conform to the norms of conventional society. Sure enough, he proves to be 'most unteachable' (30), eschewing the trappings of religion, including the rosary – a string of beads which a Catholic would use to aid concentration on prayer (31) – even though he was taught by a Friar. This interest in Catholicism and the exotic Spanish castle setting are in keeping with the **gothic** genre.

The boy's imitation of birds and knowledge of nature reveals that he is, like Wordsworth's Idiot Boy, a representative of idealised, unsocialised natural humanity. The foster-mother considers the young man to have become mentally unstable, and blames this on excessive reading (43), perhaps reflecting the prejudices of the relatively uneducated. Her comment that the youth had 'unlawful thoughts of many things' (45) can be seen in a similar light, as well

CHECK THE BOOK

It was at one time common for people to assume that natural events, especially disasters such as earthquakes, were caused by human sin. This belief is part of the story of *The Spire* (1964), a novel by William Golding set in the Middle Ages.

as expressing the views of someone who unquestioningly accepts religious dictates. Lord Velez, it seems, though inclined to philosophical enquiry, is so unnerved by the localised earthquake that occurs, that he repents their 'heretical and lawless talk' (56) and blames it all on the boy, throwing him into 'that hole' (58).

The youth's 'doleful song' (62) which Leoni overhears is very much in keeping with the philosophy of the Romantics, who tended to believe in the ideal of the 'noble savage' promulgated by the French philosopher Rousseau (see **Detailed summaries: The Dungeon**). The youth's disappearance in the newly discovered land is quixotic and romantic, but leaves the poem somewhat unresolved. We are left musing about his possible fate, but without any sense of closure. Indeed, if we imagine ourselves back with the foster-mother and Maria, we are left not with closure but with the **symbol** of the dungeon entrance – an opening leading on to unnamed possibilities.

GLOSSARY		
22	**lusty**	strong
31	**told a bead**	used a rosary for prayer
37	**simples**	medicinal herbs
63	**savannah**	open grasslands
83	**savage men**	supposedly uncivilised people, such as Native Americans

CHECK THE FILM

The image of someone disappearing up a river leading into a largely unknown continent is a powerful **metaphor** used in several films: for example, *Love in the Time of Cholera* (dir. Mike Newell, 2007, based on the novel of the same name by Gabriel García Márquez) and *Fitzcarraldo* (dir. Werner Herzog, 1982).

LINES LEFT UPON A SEAT IN A YEW-TREE

- A poet addresses the traveller, describing a remote and barren spot and the man who erected a seat there.
- We learn that the man was idealistic but rejected society when he failed to make a name for himself.
- The poet advises the traveller against similar pride.

This is an example of inscriptional poetry, a genre which has its roots in classical epitaphs, in which Wordsworth was interested. The conceit of the poem is that it is left, or inscribed, on a seat by an anonymous poet who knew the man who erected the seat, there to be read by passing travellers. It invites the traveller to rest and consider the moral lesson of the proud man who once frequented the spot. The poem is inspired by a slightly less remotely situated seat erected by the Reverend William Braithwaite, but the character described is probably only loosely based on him. The **persona** of the anonymous poet is very close to being Wordsworth himself, who would have been familiar with the real Esthwaite Water in the Lake District to which the subtitle refers.

COMMENTARY

The poem begins with the conventional plea found in classical epitaphs, before justifying a claim on the traveller's attention. The spot may lack the usual charms of places described in pastoral poetry, whose style is **parodied** in Wordsworth's 'sparkling rivulets', 'verdant herb' (3) and reference to bees, but it has a quiet beauty of its own. Its barrenness might create a similar vacancy in the traveller's mind, but there will be at least 'one soft impulse' (7) to please him in the lapping of the waves.

CHECK THE POEM

The traditional association of bees with pastoral contentment is continued by W. B. Yeats (1865–1939), who in 'The Lake Isle of Innisfree' proposes to 'live alone in the bee-loud glade'.

The conceit of the poem continues after the first break, when the poet introduces the man who is its main subject. Wordsworth catches our interest by withholding the man's identity. The **syntax** creates an expectation, then frustrates it by leaving him anonymous, ending the first sentence only with 'I well remember' (12). However, Wordsworth does paint a vivid picture of this man's decline from bold, talented, idealistic youth to proud but dejected recluse. The man is said to have launched himself upon the world like a brave knight, prepared for all enemies, but not prepared for being ignored – which is what actually happened to him. Disheartened, he consoled himself by retreating into proud disdain for the world that failed to appreciate him.

We have an image of the man choosing to envelop himself in gloom, training the dark tree to fold its arms around him, choosing shadow rather than light. The natural moorland visitors – the sheep, stone-chat and sandpiper – add charm to the picture. There is even a suggestion of welcome variety in the alteration of the **blank verse's iambic** rhythm that comes with the words 'sand-piper' and 'juniper' (24–5) (one has to stress the first syllable instead of the second). Nonetheless, the barrenness of the spot provides him with an image of his own lack of achievement. A complex character, although he is disappointed, he still appreciates the beauty of the landscape. However, it is significant that he gazes 'On the more distant scene' (31), which perhaps adds to his sense of a better life that remains beyond his reach. Similarly, when he thinks of those who see the world and humanity as being equally lovely, he does not go out and seek their companionship; rather, he indulges himself in 'mournful joy' (39), to think that others have feelings of love and kinship which he can never share. He is a victim of his own morbid imagination. The 'deep vale' (42) in which he dies is both the lakeside setting itself, the Vale of Esthwaite, and the state of gloomy introspection into which he has sunk. The fact that he leaves no monument but the seat suggests that, having cut himself off from society, he is not even missed or remembered by loved ones.

The last **stanza** of the poem contains the moral, in what is surely one of the finest philosophical statements in Wordsworth's verse, or indeed any verse. Continuing with the inscriptional **conceit**, Wordsworth issues a stern reminder:

> Stranger! henceforth be warned; and know, that pride,
> Howe'er disguised in its own majesty,
> Is littleness. (46–8)

Here the **syntax** cleverly emphasises the sense, the shortness of the sentence's concluding phrase matching the 'littleness' of the proud man. Wordsworth is spiritually radical in his insistence that every 'living thing' (49) deserves respect, and in his tacit acknowledgement that even the contemptuous individual, whose intellect is 'in its infancy' (51), might yet develop a more enlightened understanding. To Wordsworth, the self-obsessed man might move even a wise man to unwise scorn – like the proverbial individual who 'tries the patience of Job'. Wordsworth concludes that the true dignity lies in the ability to question ('suspect', 59) yet respect ('revere') oneself, in an attitude of humility.

GLOSSARY

3	**verdant herb** green grass or other growth
7	**vacancy** emptiness of mind
24	**stone-chat** a moorland bird that makes a sound like two stones banged together
24	**glancing sand-piper** a shoreline bird, darting in its movements, that nests on moorland

QUESTION

'Lines left upon a Seat in a Yew-tree' is a poem with an uncompromising moral – something less acceptable to modern taste than it was in Wordsworth's lifetime. How far do you agree with its moral, and how effective do you find the way in which it is presented here?

THE NIGHTINGALE, A CONVERSATIONAL POEM

- The poet describes hearing a nightingale's song at night.
- He reflects on how poets have referred to the nightingale as melancholy.
- He describes a place frequented by nightingales, and a young woman who appreciates them.
- He vows to expose his own son to nature, especially to the nightingale.

This poem is unusual in the collection. As its subtitle, 'A conversational poem', suggests, it wanders in a relaxed manner around its subject, moving in a conversational way from one idea to the next, rather than telling a story or describing a character. In addition, while definitely not being a **ballad**, it is more lyrical than many of the poems in this collection, having an elegant turn of phrase and a consciously poetic **diction** that many of the others lack. At the same time, its elegance is unpretentious. Coleridge himself thought that the poem declined in quality as it progressed, and indicated this in a light-hearted and rather improper piece of verse that he sent to Wordsworth along with a copy of 'The Nightingale'.

COMMENTARY

Coleridge begins with three lines which may be intended as a mild rejection of conventionally poetic images of twilight. If this is his

CHECK THE POEM

John Clare (1793–1864) also portrays the nightingale as joyous. In 'The Nightingale's Nest' he writes: 'Her wings would tremble in her ecstasy,/ And feathers stand on end, as 'twere with joy.'

intention, the lines are, nonetheless, a beautiful evocation of the last vestiges of daylight which have recently given way to night. He draws us into the poem by inviting us, along with his friends, to 'rest on this old mossy Bridge' (4) painting a sensually appealing picture of the stream below and the dim stars above. Quickly he introduces the nightingale itself, quoting Milton's line and denying that the nightingale is melancholy. He makes the very astute point that nothing in nature is melancholy, though many poets have copied Milton in ascribing this mood to the nightingale. Such poets, says Coleridge, would do better to give themselves up to the influence of nature, so that their poems 'Should make all nature lovelier' (33). Young people waste their time in ballrooms and theatres when they could be experiencing 'the deep'ning twilights of the spring' (36). The word 'deep'ning' here suggests that such experience would deepen them emotionally as well as referring to the increasing darkness of twilight. These same young people, overly influenced by 'poetical' cliché (35), sigh over the classical myth of Philomela rather than listening to real nightingales!

Coleridge asserts that he, Wordsworth and Dorothy have learned to appreciate the joy that is present in the song of the nightingale. While this is perhaps projecting human emotion on to the bird as much as Milton does, Coleridge is at least accurate in identifying the bird's song as a 'love-chant' (48) – more exactly, a mating song – rather than a mournful complaint. Despite this, the setting of the neglected and overgrown castle grove that Coleridge describes, if not quite melancholy, is certainly quite **gothic**. In keeping with this tone, the anonymous 'gentle maid' (64) who 'Glides through the pathways' (69) is almost ghostly, and the suggestion that she is a pagan priestess, dedicated to 'something more than nature' (68) is full of gothic mystery. In contrast, the sudden outburst of song from the nightingale is full of life and vigour, enhanced by the lively musical image of 'choral minstrelsy' (75) and the gale-swept 'hundred airy harps' (77).

In the last section of the poem Coleridge bids farewell to the nightingale, and to William and Dorothy, only to be drawn back again by the sound of the bird, which in turn makes him think of how much his infant son would love to hear it. The description of

CHECK THE POEM

Milton called the nightingale melancholy in his long poem 'Il Penseroso'.

the child listening with 'his hand beside his ear,/ His little hand, the small forefinger up' (89–90) is tender in its loving attention to detail. Likewise, the account of his being comforted by the moon, with its description of his eyes glittering in its light, is engaging. However, it takes the focus of the poem away from its core subject, the nightingale, and its language lacks the sheer brilliance with which the song of the nightingale is described. This is perhaps why Coleridge felt that the poem declined towards the end.

The poem is in **blank verse**, which gives it a certain quiet dignity, matched by the fairly formal and elegant diction. The language is often quite elevated compared with that of other poems in the collection which deliberately attempt to reproduce the language of the common man. This is true of the opening three lines, but we also find such words as 'verdure' (8), for green growth, and poetic phrases such as 'precipitates/ With fast thick warble his delicious notes' (45), as well as the musical **imagery** mentioned earlier.

 QUESTION

How far do you agree with Coleridge's own judgement on 'The Nightingale'? Does it begin well, then decline?

GLOSSARY	
3	**sullen** dim
18	**distemper** *dis-temper*, mental disturbance or depression
44	**precipitates** speeds up or hurries
59	**passagings** sallies, attacks, as well as musical passages; part of the idea that nightingales engage in musical competition with each other
60	**jug jug** the sound traditionally ascribed to nightingales
77	**airy harps** Aeolian harps, designed to be sounded by the wind
88	**Mars** distorts, misrepresents

CONTEXT

The American Revolutionary War (1775–83), also known as the American War of Independence, resulted from the desire of thirteen American colonies to break away from British rule. It escalated when Revolutionary France supported the American cause. Britain lost the war and carried on fighting France.

CONTEXT

The literacy of the narrator in 'The Female Vagrant' is a significant factor. Estimates of literacy rates for women in Britain for the late eighteenth century vary from thirty to fifty per cent, but for women of the narrator's class and rural background these figures would be much lower. The number of women in her position sufficiently literate to read widely for pleasure would be lower still.

THE FEMALE VAGRANT

- The narrator describes her idyllic childhood in the Lake District.
- She and her father lose their home and have to depend on her fiancé, whom she marries, bearing him three children.
- Her father dies and her husband enlists to fight in America, where he and the children die.
- The narrator sails back to England, recalling the horrors of war.
- She arrives penniless, becomes ill, recovers, and is befriended by gypsies.
- She leaves the gypsies, becomes a lone vagrant, and meets the poet.

This is a tragic tale of exploitation of the poor by the rich, mistreatment by government, the horror of war, and society's failure to prevent an honest and hard-working woman from suffering extreme hardship. The poem has a strong **narrative** thread and falls into six chronological sections, framed by the barely glimpsed **persona** of the poet-narrator, to whom the woman tells her 'artless story' (2), and who comments briefly on her sorrow at the end of the poem. Its nine-line **iambic pentameter stanzas**, consisting of two rhyming **quatrains** with an additional line added after the first, forming a **couplet**, convey a sense of dignity that adds to the narrator's tragic stature.

COMMENTARY

Stanzas 1–4 paint an idyllic picture of the narrator's early years, raised by her good, honest father on the banks of a lake in Cumbria. Although her mother must have died, as she is not mentioned, her place is taken by nature, which smiles on father and daughter: their field, flock and fishing provide them with everything they need. There is a sense of ampleness, freedom and expanse in such phrases as 'more than mines of gold', rhyming with 'transport [happiness] roll'd', 'stretch'd' and 'fleecy store' (4–8). She becomes an avid reader – a detail which would endear her to Wordsworth's early audience as much as her appreciation of the pastoral delights of stanza 3, and the neatness and consideration for passing strangers shown in stanza 4.

Into this Eden comes the serpent of privilege, in the form of the grasping master of the 'mansion proud' (39) that springs up nearby. Wordsworth may here intend special criticism for the *nouveau riche*, as opposed to the established landowning class, who in some cases at least showed some consideration for their tenants and poorer neighbours. The father's love for his 'hereditary nook' (44) is contrasted with the new landowner's greed and his assumption that he can buy everything with 'proffered gold' (46). This landowner either causes the downturn in the father's fortunes or takes advantage of it. It is perhaps because of her consciousness of this exploitation that the narrator (like the Ancient Mariner) finds herself unable to pray (62).

In the next section of the poem, in stanzas 8–10, we meet the narrator's sweetheart and are briefly returned to the pastoral idyll in her recollection of hours spent with him in the mountains singing 'like little birds in May' (66–7) before he had to leave to become an artisan in a town. Now, however, the narrator's misfortunes produce a temporary silver lining to this cloud, when they reunite her with her fiancé. Strangely, no marriage is mentioned, but she refers to him in stanza 11 as her husband. It is important to the reader's sympathy with her that the family's 'daily bread' is 'By constant toil and constant prayer supplied', the repetition of 'constant' emphasising her and her husband's worthiness. This is a happy interlude, but the narrator's unexplained sighs (85–6) prepare us for the sorrows to come.

Wordsworth uses well-chosen physical details to represent phases in the story, keeping it alive in our minds without the necessity of describing every twist and turn of a decline that spans many years. Thus we see 'The empty loom, cold hearth, and silent wheel' (89) of unemployment, the 'proud parade, the noisy drum' (93) of the

CONTEXT

In the late eighteenth century, handloom weavers were losing work to factories in industrial cities. At the same time, the factory owners were becoming part of a newly wealthy class. The man who in effect forces the narrator's family from their home could well be part of this class.

CONTEXT

Someone in the position of the woman in 'The Female Vagrant' could expect little help from the state, despite being a war widow. At best she could expect to be placed in a workhouse, where conditions were harsh and there was little chance of returning to the outside community.

CHECK THE POEM

One example of **Romantic personification** is 'Ode on Melancholy', by John Keats (1795–1821): 'She dwells with Beauty – Beauty that must die;/ And Joy, whose hand is ever at his lips/ Bidding adieu; and aching Pleasure nigh.'

recruiting officers, and hear that 'no knell was heard' (104) for those who die, **ironically** within sight of 'Green fields … and our native shore' (102), while waiting for the troop ship to leave port. Poor and exploited, they are not even given a church burial.

Grim though the stormy crossing of the Atlantic is, those who reach 'the western world' (America) have such a 'harvest of affliction' in store that they wish they had not survived (115–16). This homely **metaphor** is bitterly ironic, since a harvest normally sustains. Wordsworth initially presents the horrors of war through **imagery** that is unusually vivid for *Lyrical Ballads*, especially in the **personification** of abstractions. Thus the **narrator** says that it would be better to die (of starvation) in 'Want's most lonely cave' (120) than to survive on the suffering of others, 'dog-like, wading [as if in a sea of blood] at the heels of war' (124). Even more arresting is the image of the scavengers lapping 'their brother's blood' (126).

It is concordant with Wordsworth's poetic philosophy of portraying 'emotion recollected in tranquillity' that the woman describes the actual details of war as recollections that seem to come to her while on board a ship carrying her back to England (stanzas 17–18). Thus we read of the 'festering heaps' of bodies (147) and 'The shriek that from the distant battle broke' (149). In the face of such almost indescribable horrors, Wordsworth also once again (as in lines 120–6) resorts to personification of abstractions, very much in the style of the Augustan poets whose style he was trying to leave behind:

CONTEXT

Wordsworth was very much opposed to Britain's waging war on Revolutionary France, and this is probably reflected in the sentiments expressed in 'The Female Vagrant' regarding the war with the American colonies. See, too, **Background: William Wordsworth** for more on his affair with Annette Vallon in France.

And Fire from Hell reared his gigantic shape,
And Murder, by the ghastly gleam, and Rape
Seized their joint prey … (157–9)

He uses the calmness of the sea as an emotional foil to these horrors, rather as Coleridge uses the sea to reflect emotion in *The Rime of the Ancyent Marinere*. It is invested with an almost mystical silence, strikingly expressed in the line 'I looked and looked along the silent air' (143), expressing the process by which the narrator recovers a sense of equilibrium. There are also echoes of Coleridge in the repetition used to emphasise the narrator's dire situation when she finally comes ashore:

And homeless near a thousand homes I stood,
And near a thousand tables pined, and wanted food.
(179–80)

A plain but effective **simile** is used to describe the narrator's plight: 'Helpless as sailor cast on desart rock' (183). She is helpless not only because she is penniless and grief-stricken, but because she lacks the experience or moral indifference to beg or steal: 'Nor to the beggar's language could I frame my tongue' (189). She becomes ill, but even in hospital she meets 'careless cruelty' (205). Ironically, it is when she is discharged and meets a band of gypsies that she encounters kindness and generosity for the first time since leaving England. It was radical of Wordsworth to introduce this idea, since gypsies were generally viewed with fear and suspicion. The gypsy life is portrayed with romantic idealism, although this is partly a reflection of the gypsies' self-portrayal:

… the yellow sheaf
In every vale for their delight was stowed:
For them, in nature's meads, the milky udder flowed.
(223–5)

In other words, they stole corn and milk from farmers! The darker truth is revealed when the narrator gives her reasons for leaving her gypsy friends: she is too moral to be happy aiding and abetting their criminal activities (stanza 27).

As the poem nears its end, the narrator describes her life leading up to the moment when she meets the poet and tells her story. When she considers her routine hardships, what she feels with keenest remorse is that she has 'abused' her 'inner self' (259) by at least occasionally resorting to falsehood in order to survive. After all that she has suffered, this is evidence indeed of her true nobility, which makes her tale all the more poignant. When she weeps, finally, it is because even telling her tale to this stranger is not enough to lighten the load 'which on her spirit lay' (270).

CHECK THE POEM

Compare Wordsworth's use of repetition with Coleridge's in *The Rime of the Ancyent Marinere*, for example in lines 224–5: 'Alone, alone, all, all alone,/ Alone on a wide wide sea!'

CHECK THE BOOK

Jane Austen presents gypsies as a shadowy threat to mainstream society in *Emma* (1815), in which they threaten Emma's friend Harriet Smith.

CONTEXT

Even in the late eighteenth century the Protestant work ethic was strong, though it became more of a feature of social policy for the Victorians. Those opposed to offering the poor more assistance often argued that they had only themselves to blame.

CHECK THE BOOK

Novelist, poet and traveller George Borrow (1803–81) lived with gypsies for some time and wrote sympathetically about them and their lifestyle in his novels *Lavengro* (1851) and *Romany Rye* (1857).

CONTEXT

In his 1802 Preface, Wordsworth writes: '… personifications of abstract ideas rarely occur in these volumes and, I hope, are utterly rejected as an ordinary device to elevate the style, and raise it above Prose.' He presumably felt that the horror of war justified their use in 'The Female Vagrant'.

GLOSSARY

1	Derwent's side by Wordsworth's own footnote to line 51, the banks of Derwent Water, a lake in the Lake District, though it could also refer to the River Derwent
3	flood the lake (or river)
23	gambols and wild freaks probably the leaping and struggling of sheep trying to escape the shearer, though it could refer to human festivities
43	gainsay oppose, deny
44	hereditary nook a secluded little inherited dwelling
48	Sore-traversed severely thwarted or done down
50	substance material wealth or means of support
74	artist's trade skilled manual worker's craft
89	wheel spinning wheel: there was no work
92	relief possibly financial aid under the provisions of the Poor Law
95	strain embrace
103	fever, from polluted air incurred in Wordsworth's time it was thought that disease came from miasmas, or polluted air
110	equinoctial deep stormy sea; the fleet has missed the calm of summer; the weather is often unsettled around the autumn equinox
117	devoted doomed
120	Want deprivation
138	main sea
145	terrific terrifying
150	the mine's dire earthquake the explosion caused by an explosive device placed in a siege tunnel
183	morsel morsel (a misprint)
191	the crowd's resort resorting to begging from the crowd
197	interruption short … sense short spells of anguished consciousness
223	wain cart
226	Semblance … door to door they looked like, or posed as, travelling potters with donkeys carrying straw-lined baskets
231	uplighted lit up
247	marriage such as mine her husband's family probably disapproved of her and would be reluctant to help her
265	this moor in Wordsworth's original conception, Salisbury Plain

GOODY BLAKE AND HARRY GILL

- The poem introduces Harry Gill, a farmer who can never get warm.
- His vigour is compared with the age and poverty of Goody Blake.
- She takes firewood from Harry's hedge, and one day Gill catches her.
- She prays that he will never again feel warm, and he never does.

This **ballad** is Wordsworth's retelling of an apparently true story related by Erasmus Darwin as an example of what might now be called a psychosomatic illness – one caused by the sufferer's beliefs. Wordsworth may well have seen the story in a similar light, but it also fits into a folk tradition of curses pronounced by slighted or injured women (the tale of *Sleeping Beauty* is a variant of this.) There is also a moral implied: Harry Gill's coldness of character – his lack of generosity – is punished by coldness of body. Goody Blake, like Simon Lee in 'Simon Lee, the old Huntsman', is old and extremely poor. She is one of Wordsworth's examples of suffering humanity oppressed by someone in a more powerful position. However, her response to her plight is not like Simon Lee's. Confronted by the man who would deny her a few sticks for a fire to warm herself on a freezing winter's night, she calls on a higher power, in effect cursing Harry Gill and condemning him to feel as cold as her for ever.

COMMENTARY

This is a fairly simple ballad of **stanzas** consisting of paired **quatrains** of **iambic quadrameter**. The rhymed and frequently **end-stopped** lines increase its earthy folk ballad quality. However, there is one **metrical** subtlety, namely the extra unstressed syllable at the end of the first and third lines of each stanza, resulting in a **feminine rhyme**. This gives a livelier feeling to the poem, preventing it from becoming pedestrian.

CONTEXT

Erasmus Darwin (1731–1802) was a physician and philosopher. In his book, *Zoönomia* (1794–6), he anticipates the work of his grandson Charles Darwin in a way which would appeal to Wordsworth, suggesting '… that all warm-blooded animals have arisen from one living filament, which the great First Cause endued with animality, with the power of acquiring new parts, attended with new propensities, directed by irritations, sensations, volitions and associations, and thus possessing the faculty of continuing to improve by its own inherent activity.'

The language of the poem, matching the **ballad** form, is rustic and rarely surprising. The description of Harry as a 'lusty drover', 'stout of limb', with cheeks 'red as ruddy clover' (19–20) is quite conventional (and 'ruddy' means 'red'). Nor do the phrases describing Goody Blake as 'old and poor;/ Ill fed … and thinly clad' (22) distinguish her in any way from any number of poor old women. The description of the summer day as 'lightsome' (38) is slightly unusual, as is the line 'But when the ice our streams did fetter' (41), the word 'fetter' neatly suggesting both the imprisonment of the streams and Goody Blake's confinement to her bed by the cold.

CONTEXT

Regarding the 'trespass of old Goody Blake' (66), there was controversy over whether the gathering of firewood by the poor was a traditional right or a crime. The law increasingly tended to regard it as theft.

The fact that a stormy night is welcome to Goody Blake as it leaves firewood for her to gather underlines the extent of her poverty. The use of the word 'alluring' does the same in a faintly **ironic** way in the **rhetorical** question:

> Could any thing be more alluring
> Than an old hedge to Goody Blake? (59–60)

An 'old hedge' is a prosaic and unromantic thing to be described in this way! It seems therefore very small-minded and mean of Harry Gill to be so intent on catching the old woman and depriving her of warmth – especially when it means he has to wait at night himself, in the cold, in order to catch her.

There is a wonderful piece of story-telling suspense in lines 73–80. Wordsworth sets the scene: moonlight, 'And crisp with frost the stubble land'. He then shifts to the immediacy of the present tense, with the short, tense phrases and the one-word question putting us in the shoes of Harry Gill:

> – He hears a noise – he's all awake –
> Again? – on tip-toe down the hill
> He softly creeps –

The climax of the poem comes in the next **stanza** when the young drover catches the old woman. There is a kind of mock-epic quality in the repetitions and **alliteration** of this stanza: 'fiercely by the arm

… by the arm he held her fast'. Goody Blake, however, gets her revenge straight away. Her curse of coldness is linked to the 'cold, cold moon above her head'.

The old woman is not mentioned during the remaining three stanzas, during which the focus is all on Harry Gill's vain attempts to get warm. There is another homespun though effective **simile** in his teeth 'clattering' 'Like a loose casement in the wind' (116). We hear yet again that his teeth 'chatter, chatter still' (126, as in 3–4 and 12). The 'lusty drover' (17) has become as pathetic a figure as the old woman herself.

> ? **QUESTION**
>
> Do you regard Harry Gill as the victim of a witch-like curse or of his own superstition or sense of guilt?

GLOSSARY

17	**drover**	one who rears cattle and drives them to market
21	**Goody**	Housewife
31	**country**	area
33	**pottage**	a boiled dish of oatmeal or vegetables
39	**canty**	cheerful, healthy
66	**trespass**	crime or misdemeanour

LINES WRITTEN AT A SMALL DISTANCE FROM MY HOUSE

- The poet invites his sister to join him outside in the spring sunshine and spend the day in idleness.

This is a poem vigorously expressing Wordsworth's delight in the joys of a mild spring morning and asking his sister to join him. Like 'Expostulation and Reply' and its companion 'The Tables Turned', it praises sensory experience of nature over intellect and book-learning. Although Wordsworth names the boy messenger as his friend Basil Montagu's son, it is likely that the idea of his writing and sending the poem as an invitation to his sister is something of a **conceit**, albeit a charming one, given the speed with which Wordsworth urges his sister to join him: a short note would have been quicker!

>  **CHECK THE POEM**
>
> Another poem which rejoices in the first signs of spring is John Clare's 'February: A Thaw' (*Selected Poems and Prose*, OUP).

COMMENTARY

This poem is one of a handful in *Lyrical Ballads* that are unusual in expressing pure joy from start to finish. It twice acknowledges that this 'idleness' will last only 'for this one day' (15–16, 39–40), yet proposes that this day will set the tone for the rest of the year. Indeed, the whole poem is about beginnings. It is the beginning of spring, and nature is full of promise: 'There is a blessing in the air' (5) despite the 'bare trees' and 'mountains bare' (7). Wordsworth proposes that he and his sister should begin their nature-based calendar on this day.

The poem is also about feeling, both in the sensory and the emotional sense. It appeals to the senses, with its evocation of the robin's song (3), the sights of nature, and its urging Dorothy to 'Come forth and feel the sun' (12), but it also refers to 'the hour of feeling' (24) in which they may become deeply attuned to nature, and thus to love itself as a universal principle. Wordsworth tells Dorothy to put on her 'woodland dress' (14), which at a simple level merely suggests suitable outdoor clothing, but which also implies a celebration of spring, and of nature. Wordsworth expresses his belief that exposure to nature produces harmony in human beings, and that this harmony encourages them to love one another.

The connection between body and soul is emphasised by the lines 'Our minds shall drink at every pore/ The spirit of the season' (27–8). This **metaphor** suggests that the mind can simply absorb the health-giving energy of nature. Moreover, nature produces the 'silent laws' (29) of a morality whose basis is love, and which stems ultimately from 'the blessed power' (33) which is all around: this is Wordsworth at his most obviously **pantheistic**. Yet rather than producing a mood of solemn awe, the poem has the lightness of music and dance. Echoed phrases such as 'From earth to man, from man to earth' (23) are musical, as is the idea of souls being 'tuned' to love (36). Similarly, the phrase 'frame the measure' (35) suggests dance.

The **iambic metre** and simple *abab* rhyme scheme also create a liveliness that reflects the energetic mood of the poem. The short fourth line of each **stanza** seems to drive it home, as if Wordsworth's persuasive argument is irresistible.

SIMON LEE, THE OLD HUNTSMAN

- The narrator tells of a former huntsman, now aged and frail.
- His work has left him one-eyed, half-crippled and unskilled.
- Simon and his wife can barely survive.
- The narrator relates helping Simon to uproot a tree stump, and how he was affected by the old man's great gratitude.

Wordsworth describes an old man who has dedicated his active life to serving the aristocracy as a 'running huntsman' (14). Although once famed for his hunting exploits and enthusiasm, his work has left him physically ruined. Moreover, as a huntsman, he has never developed the skills that would help him and his wife to survive on a meagre smallholding. With no benefactor or children, his days are numbered. Wordsworth tells how, with only a little effort, he helped the old man to uproot a tree stump. The poet is quietly outraged that this man, who has served the aristocracy so well, and in a merely recreational pursuit rather than in some more worthwhile way, nonetheless has so little to show for it that he is pathetically grateful for such slight assistance.

COMMENTARY

The poem is written loosely in **ballad** style, in stanzas consisting of two **quatrains** each, although they deviate from the norm in their unrhymed fifth and seventh lines. The ballad form befits the homely subject, as does the simple and unadorned diction. The sole image, 'His cheek is like a cherry' (16), is in keeping with the homespun, unsophisticated character of both man and poem. Wordsworth paints a picture of a man, once tall, worn down in stature by the excessive demands made on his body, and by later suffering. There is some suggestion that despite having 'but one eye left' (15) he is still cheerful, if we can assume that being cherry-cheeked implies this.

There is considerable pathos in the fact that someone renowned 'four counties round' (19) has been reduced to such pitiful circumstances. Simon's old master is dead and the 'hall of Ivor' (22) is now uninhabited – though there is no guarantee, or suggestion from the poet, that Simon would have been given more support were this not the case. Wordsworth contrasts the man's former fame and glee (18–19) with his present state. Lines 33–5, especially, spell out this sad contrast. The phrase 'little body' conveys Wordsworth's pity for the man, and the down-to-earth rhyming of 'And he is lean and he is sick' with 'His ankles they are swoln and thick' emphasises his physical condition.

In stanza 6 we see a probable reason for Simon's infirmity being so extreme. The fact that he often 'reeled and was stone-blind' (44) suggests that even in his hey-day he almost killed himself in his determination to keep going. The fact that his heart rejoices when he hears the hounds is an enduring proof of the 'glee' (18) that he once felt in his work, but it is also **ironic**, given what that work has done to him. Each **stanza** adds a further sense of the old couple's difficulties. The repeated phrase 'scrap of land' (59) emphasises how little the old couple have, but even this is of little use to them now that they have no strength to farm it.

Wordsworth employs the conventional epithet in directly addressing the 'gentle' reader (69), yet there is the added suggestion that the reader is likely to be 'gentle' in class, and therefore better off than Simon Lee. Wordsworth is perhaps playing with this idea of the reader's relative good fortune when he confesses that what he has to say is not much of a tale. The privileged reader will require 'Such stores as silent thought can bring' (74) to appreciate the tale of upper-class exploitation of the poor implied by Simon Lee's condition.

The poet ends the poem with a reflection on his own emotional response to Simon's excessive gratitude. He is left mourning 'the gratitude of men' (103) for the scraps of comfort thrown them by others in a world that has treated them unjustly. Whereas Simon Lee himself is uncomplaining, Wordsworth feels both compassion and moral indignation.

 **QUESTION**

How do you regard Wordsworth's apparent attitude towards Simon Lee, given that the old man himself does not complain about his lot, and evidently enjoyed his work – as is suggested by the way 'his heart rejoices' (46) when he hears the hounds?

GLOSSARY

6	**burthen** burden
9	**livery-coat** servant's uniform identifying his master's house
14	**running huntsman** one whose job involved following the hunt on foot
34	**awry** out of alignment, crooked
51	**stout** strong
85	**mattock** spade-like tool used to grub up tree roots
89	**overtasked** faced with too difficult a task for you

ANECDOTE FOR FATHERS

- The narrator describes walking with his young son and asking him which he prefers – their former home or their new one.
- The boy says he prefers their old home, then gives as his reason the fact that the new one has no weather-cock.

Wordsworth probably intended this as a companion piece to 'We Are Seven', which also features a child being insistently quizzed by an adult, with a moral being implied from the answers given by the child. Wordsworth, who actually had no son of his own at this time, identifies the boy (named 'Edward' in the poem) as the five-year-old Basil Montagu, the son of a friend. The poem's **narrator** describes asking his son which place he prefers. The child's discomfort at being pressed for an explanation was obviously crucial to Wordsworth, as **stanza** 12, in which it is expressed, was reworked several times in later editions.

COMMENTARY

In both this poem and 'We Are Seven' an adult insistently and rather insensitively puts questions to a child. The lesson of both poems lies in the fact that the questions are in a sense meaningless to the child, as a child's consciousness is different from that of the adult. The girl in 'We Are Seven' lacks an adult's understanding of death; in 'Anecdote

CONTEXT

While living at Racedown, Dorset, William and Dorothy were paid £50 a year to look after the son of their friend Basil Montagu. They worried about how to stop him telling lies. They concluded that it was their own questions that were to blame.

CHECK THE POEM

William Blake (1757–1827) wrote a number of poems in his *Songs of Innocence and of Experience* in which he explored the responsibility of the parent to the innocent child; for example, 'The Little Boy Lost': 'Father, father, where are you going?/ O do not walk so fast!/ Speak, father, speak to your little boy,/ Or else I shall be lost.'

for Fathers' the child responds from a purely emotional standpoint, rather than a logical one. It is not in his childish nature to make an analytical comparison of the two places and explain his preference rationally, yet that is what the father demands of him – five times (47)! The world of reasoning is barely within his comprehension, yet he does his best to satisfy his father, producing an almost random explanation, since he understands that one is required. This, presumably, is what the **narrator** says in the last **stanza** he has learned from the incident. By making an unreasonable demand of the child, he has, as the poem's subtitle indicates, encouraged him to make up a lie.

The poem compares adult and childish consciousness in other ways. The father thinks of 'former pleasures' (9), and is aware of the passing of time, as shown especially by the repetition in 'A long, long year before' (12). The child, one assumes, lives in the present moment – like the 'young lambs' racing each other in the sunshine (21). Similarly, the father remembers being happy on this day, but the very fact of his stating that he '… could bear/ To think, and think, and think again' (9–10), and 'I could not feel a pain' (12), suggests that this day was unusual, and that on other days he could not bear to think, and could indeed feel pain. Likewise, whereas the boy simply expresses his feelings, to the father, these must be justified: 'There surely must some reason be' (42).

The poem differs from 'We Are Seven', however, in that the father here appears to learn from his son's replies: the adult in 'We Are Seven' is left apparently baffled by the girl's attitude. It may also be that there is a further lesson in 'Anecdote for Fathers' to be found in the image of the weather-cock. It is 'gilded' (52), suggesting something that is only superficially bright. This in turn implies deception, as could the fact that a weather-cock changes position with the wind. There could even be a pun on the 'vane' and 'vain'. It is vain for the father to expect a reasoned answer from his son.

GLOSSARY	
7	**intermitted** intermittent, occasional rather than constant
10	**Kilve** a village on the Bristol Channel, near Alfoxden
58	**lore** teaching

WE ARE SEVEN

- The narrator asks a child how many children are in her family.
- She says there are seven, and he asks where the others are.
- Although two are in Conway, two at sea, and two are dead, she will not be shaken from her count of seven.

After an initial question from the **narrator** to an imaginary brother, and a description of the 'cottage girl' (5), the poem consists of a dialogue between the narrator and the girl. She numbers herself and her siblings, insisting on there being seven of them altogether, despite the fact that two are dead. This could be seen as a sentimental view, but Wordsworth seems to be making a more profound comment on the child's inability to comprehend death.

COMMENTARY

Wordsworth begins with a question that informs the whole of the poem. The narrator asks, more or less **rhetorically**, what a child who is untroubled by thoughts of personal mortality, and whose experience is dominated by a strong sense of vitality, should understand of death. The rest of the poem answers that question.

The girl is unsophisticated, 'a little cottage girl', with a 'rustic, woodland air' and 'wildly clad' (5, 9–10). This identifies her as a child of nature, preoccupied with her own strongly flowing life force. Even her thick, curly hair and beautiful eyes reinforce this. When the narrator asks her, conversationally, how many are in the family, she includes the dead sister and brother, just as she does those absent for other reasons. She volunteers the information that they 'in the churchyard lie' (21), repeating this phrase ten lines later, apparently seeing this as a different kind of life. Significantly, she does not use the word 'dead' to describe them, and the greenness of their graves points to her view that they are still in a sense living. So, too, does the fact that she goes and eats her supper with them, and even sings to them (44), as if they could hear her.

 CHECK THE POEM

Compare the 'wildly clad' (10) girl in 'We Are Seven' with the boy in 'The Foster-Mother's Tale', who is found 'wrapt in mosses' (25) and grows to be 'A pretty boy, but most unteachable' (30).

 CHECK THE BOOK

Charles Dickens's *Great Expectations* (1861) opens with a child who first learns something of his parents and brothers from their gravestones. However, Pip does not regard them as still living in the way that the girl in 'We Are Seven' does.

One might imagine that the child is, in the language of psychology, 'in denial', but lines 53–60 make it clear that this is not quite the case. She says 'The first that died was little Jane' (49), seeing her death as a merciful release from suffering. However, Jane 'went away' (52), rather than ceasing to exist, or even going to heaven – as the narrator suggests in the last two **stanzas**. The child's brother John, similarly, 'was forced to go' (59). Her very healthy focus on her own vitality is shown by the fact that both deaths are associated with play. She and her brother played round Jane's grave, and she recalls John's death as being in winter, at a time when she could 'run and slide' (58).

The simple *abab* rhyme scheme and **iambic metre** fit the child's simple view. The return to the narrator's viewpoint is matched in the final stanza by the addition of a line, in his frustrated assertion that 'those two are dead!' (65) and by an alteration in the rhyme scheme to *abccb*. The narrator's rather insensitive insistence that 'ye are only five' (36) is ultimately matched by the child's determination to retain her viewpoint.

LINES WRITTEN IN EARLY SPRING

- The poet is moved by joyful contemplation of nature to think of the inhumanity of man.

CHECK THE POEM

In some poems by the Brontë sisters the contemplation of beauty in nature turns to sadness. See for example, Anne Brontë's 'Lines written at Thorp Green', in which she regrets that the beauties of spring 'Must droop and die away' before she can return home.

Wordsworth describes how he sat in a wood in spring allowing himself to experience the delights of nature all around him. This moved him to mourn the way in which, by contrast, human beings have created a world of suffering.

COMMENTARY

The poem relates to 'Expostulation and Reply' and 'The Tables Turned', among others. In these poems, Wordsworth argues the case for allowing oneself to be simply receptive to nature; in 'Lines written in Early Spring', he describes being in this state of receptivity, and how the sweet contemplation of nature leads him to mourn what human beings have made of themselves, and, by implication, how they treat each other. His receptive state is indicated by the opening line. Instead of identifying the songs of individual species of bird, he speaks of 'a thousand blended notes'. He has entered a state in which he is simply experiencing his sensations, with little intervening thought to dull them or distance him from them.

The form of the poem matches the sense of harmony that nature creates in Wordsworth. It is in **iambic** rhymed stanzas, with the last line of each a beat shorter than the other lines, which gives each stanza a sense of completion. The language has an elegant simplicity, and the use of **enjambment** helps to avoid any sense of triteness that might otherwise be produced by the regular **metre** and rhyme scheme.

Wordsworth **personifies** nature as female, and sees 'her' as linking her manifestations to his human soul, so that he enters a state of natural harmony. The implication of stanza 2 is that human society has lost this harmony and is at odds with itself. The sense of natural harmony is built on in the next three stanzas, in each of which we see creatures of nature apparently taking pleasure in their existence. Primroses and periwinkles happily coexist, and inspire in Wordsworth the thought that each flower takes an individual pleasure in 'the air it breathes' (12). Each movement of the birds, likewise, seems to embody 'a thrill of pleasure' (16). Even the twigs are seen as actively attempting to 'catch the breezy air' (18), and taking pleasure in it. Wordsworth says that he cannot help but ascribe these feelings of pleasure to natural things: 'I must think, do all I can' (19); 'If I these thoughts may not prevent' (21). By presenting his views in this way, Wordsworth is acknowledging that he has no proof, but is relying solely on his feelings. Nonetheless they are the foundation of his 'creed' (22).

Wordsworth ends the poem with a question to the reader which reuses the phrase from the end of stanza 2: 'What man has made of man' (8). This echoes Robert Burns's reflection on 'Man's inhumanity to Man' in 'Man was made to Mourn, a Dirge' (1786).

CHECK THE POEM

'Lines written in Early Spring' could be compared with 'Lines left upon a Seat in a Yew-tree', in which the poem's subject is moved by natural beauty to mournful thoughts, but of a self-pitying rather than humanitarian kind.

CHECK THE POEM

Anne Brontë's poem 'The Bluebell' expresses a similar belief in the individual spirit, and even consciousness, of a flower to that found in 'Lines written in Early Spring': 'A fine and subtle spirit dwells/ In every little flower,/ Each one its own sweet feeling breathes/ With more or less of power.'

GLOSSARY

10	periwinkle an evergreen plant with blue flowers
22	creed a statement of belief, especially in the Christian faith

THE LAST OF THE FLOCK

- The narrator describes meeting a man tearfully carrying a lamb.
- The man tells how he built up a flock of fifty sheep from one ewe, and then was forced to sell them one by one to feed his family.

This is a poem with a simple **narrative**. The **narrator**, who is not given any real character, comments on the unusual circumstance of meeting a full-grown healthy man weeping on the public highway in England. The man then explains the reason for his distress: he has built up a flock of sheep and then been obliged to sell them one at a time to buy food for his family. The man describes the negative effect of this on his mental outlook.

COMMENTARY

 QUESTION

How much sympathy do you feel with the shepherd in 'The Last of the Flock'?

It is hard to be as sympathetic towards the shepherd as one might be towards many of Wordsworth's characters. He has not been abandoned or bereaved like Martha Ray, exploited and left sick and weak like Simon Lee, nor forced to steal sticks from a hedge to keep warm, like Goody Blake. He is healthy and strong, probably no more than middle-aged, and has lost sheep, not loved ones. True, he has been denied poor relief, but he gives no explanation for his hardship beyond having too many children to feed – and he has his flock of sheep as a resource. One might wonder why he did not breed more sheep or have fewer children, or even ask why the family didn't eat the occasional sheep instead of selling it to buy 'bread' (48)!

Of more interest is the effect that the gradual dwindling of his flock has on him. It meant much more to him than a means of earning a living. He regrets 'the end of all my gains' (36) rather than the suffering of his family. His description of losing the sheep is intense: 'Like blood-drops from my heart they dropped' (64). His grief at the steady decline in their numbers is conveyed by the repeated line 'For me it was a woeful day', each time rhymed with 'away' (60, 70, 80). One can see the poem as a study in unhealthy attachment: the man himself admits to contemplating both crime and abandonment of his family in reaction to this loss (71–80).

His near-obsession with the flock is conveyed by it being as dear to him as his children (82), whom he loved more and more so long as the flock increased, but less and less as it decreased. He never mentions his wife, and even his children seem less important to him than his sheep. He takes no comfort in the survival of his children. Indeed, with the monosyllabic rhyming **couplet** with which the poem ends, it seems that his life has ended now that he is about to lose his last sheep. This is a poem not so much about a family's bad luck and hardship as about the negative effect of a preoccupation with accumulating goods.

THE DUNGEON

- The poet bemoans the evil influence of prisons.
- He recommends exposure to the influence of nature as an alternative.

This polemical poem, dropped from later editions of *Lyrical Ballads*, is apparently inspired by a dungeon, but presents a considered argument against prison in general as a means of correction. It proposes that criminals should instead be exposed to the benign influence of nature, which would harmonise them with the world and make it impossible for them to continue on a path of crime. Though some might now see this view as idealistic and even naïve, it was radically progressive at the time in that it identified the role of environment in crime and recognised the criminal as a fellow human being who had gone astray and could be rehabilitated.

CHECK THE POEM

A very different poem about a shepherd is 'Peasant', by R. S. Thomas (1913–2000), who writes of Iago Prytherch, 'Just an ordinary man of the bald Welsh hills,/ Who pens a few sheep in a gap in the cloud.' Wordsworth's poem 'Michael', in later editions of *Lyrical Ballads*, is also about a shepherd.

CONTEXT

Crime was increasing at the end of the eighteenth century as a result of the Industrial Revolution and the large cities it created. This led to a growing interest in crime prevention. The Penitentiary Act of 1779 made imprisonment the main form of punishment, and the concept of rehabilitation began to enter government thinking on the role of prisons.

COMMENTARY

The serious purpose of this poem is reflected in Coleridge's choice of **blank verse** rather than a **ballad** format. In fact, it could not be a ballad as it has no specific story to tell. It does, however, paint a vivid picture of the general decline of the prisoner. Coleridge begins with an **ironic** comment on 'our love and wisdom' (2) in imprisoning 'each poor brother' (3). He argues that most may be innocent, but that, even for the guilty, prison is hardly a cure. His moral indignation is felt in the exclamation 'Merciful God!' (5), in the **alliteration** of 'Each pore .../ parching poverty' (6–7), and in the language of disgust: 'stagnate and corrupt ... poison/ ... loathsome plague-spot' (9–10). Those responsible for setting up and maintaining the prison system are condemned as 'pamper'd mountebanks' (11).

In a few phrases, Coleridge creates a wonderfully concise impression of the grimness of prison life, especially in 'groaning and tears,/ And savage faces, at the clanking hour' (13–14), these faces presumably being those of the unsympathetic gaolers. The assumption is very much the **Romantic** one: that human beings are by nature fundamentally good, but are corrupted by society. Thus the mould into which the virtuous 'essence' of the prisoner was poured at birth is 'hopelessly deformed' by prison life (17–19).

The second part of the poem creates an entirely different atmosphere, evoking the health-giving influence of nature. Here the alliteration is mellifluous and adds to the simple and appealing picture created: 'Thy melodies of woods, and winds, and waters' (24). The power of nature is said to be so strong that under its influence the former criminal 'can no more endure' (25) to be out of tune with natural harmony. The **imagery** is of musical harmony; nature is seen as 'general dance and minstrelsy' (27). In Coleridge's vision, the wrong-doer's 'angry spirit' (29) cannot resist becoming calm.

CHECK THE BOOK

French philosopher Jean-Jacques Rousseau had a considerable influence on Wordsworth, Coleridge and other Romantics. He believed that human beings were fundamentally good, but were corrupted by society. See for example his *The Discourses and Other Early Political Writings*, trans. Victor Gourevitch (Cambridge University Press, 1997). Rousseau was probably influenced by John Locke's concept of the *tabula rasa* – the blank slate of the child's mind on which life's impressions are made – suggesting that crime is a product of nurture rather than nature.

GLOSSARY	
11	**mountebanks** swindlers

THE MAD MOTHER

- The poet describes a wild-looking mother with a baby.
- The woman reassures her baby that she is not mad.
- She says she is married to the baby's father, but cannot find him.
- She says she and the baby will live happily in the woods.

This is a study of a mother who, if not actually insane, has certainly been mentally disturbed in the past and still shows signs of it. Dark-skinned and black-haired, she comes from overseas, and may be partly Native American, in which case her plight can be seen as a criticism of colonialism. Her promise to make 'an Indian bower', using 'the leaves that make the softest bed' (55–6) suggests a familiarity with Native American lore: if she were wholly Native American she would perhaps not identify it as 'Indian'. In addition she speaks English and says her breast has changed in 'hue', presumably from the sun (63). She has no home or means of support, and her optimism regarding her own and her child's chances of survival is probably unrealistic. The poem thus has much in common with other poems by Wordsworth about motherhood and ordinary people in desperately deprived circumstances.

COMMENTARY

An obvious question in considering this poem is the woman's actual mental state. The title, of course, is unambiguous, and her 'wild' eyes (1) seem to confirm her mental instability. She acknowledges that others call her mad, but claims that her happiness – even when singing sad songs – proves that she is not (12–14). However, the fact that she feels a need to tell her baby repeatedly not to fear her (15–16) is worrying: for most mothers this would be unnecessary. Nor is her account of her previous mental state very reassuring. She had 'a fire' in her brain and saw 'fiendish faces' hanging on her breasts, then woke and found her baby there (21–3). When later she suddenly asks her child 'Where art thou gone …/ What wicked looks are those I see?' (85–6) one fears that the 'fiendish faces' are returning and that she may mistakenly harm her child.

CHECK THE BOOK

Klaus Doerner's *Madmen and the Bourgeoisie: A Social History of Insanity and Psychiatry* (Blackwell, 1981) offers an interesting analysis of class-related attitudes towards insanity, suggesting that to some extent the concept of insanity is a bourgeois creation.

CHECK THE BOOK

Regarding the dark skin of Wordsworth's 'mad mother', there was a tendency in literature of the time, and during the nineteenth century, to associate mental instability, especially in women, with race, and to equate racial difference with 'otherness'. The Caribbean Bertha Mason in Charlotte Brontë's *Jane Eyre* is often cited as an example of this. *Wide Sargasso Sea* (1966), by Jean Rhys, expands on her story. See also Gilbert and Gubar's influential critical work *The Madwoman in the Attic* (1979).

CHECK THE POEM

'The Song of Wandering Aengus' by W. B. Yeats (1865–1939) echoes line 21 of 'The Mad Mother': 'I went out to the hazel wood,/ Because a fire was in my head.'

On the other hand, at least one aspect of her 'wildness' is her connection to nature. She wanders in the woods, and has no fear of 'the sea rock's edge', 'The high crag' and the 'leaping torrents when they howl' (45–7). She tells her child that she will be his guide 'Through hollow snows and rivers wide' (54). However, all this is double-edged: she tells her child not to 'dread the waves below' (43) but the very fact that she contemplates exposing the baby to such dangers, and feels a need to reassure him, makes us wonder how safe he is in her care. This is all the more so for her reliance on him for her own safety. It is supposedly the baby who prevents the 'high crag' from harming her, and saves her soul (46–8).

The mother, indeed, needs the baby almost as much as he needs her. She thinks he has saved her from insanity (25–6), his breast-feeding relieves her of the heartache that she experiences as a 'tight and deadly band' (31–8). Moreover, the baby has taken the place of its father in her affections (61–2). She insists that she is the father's 'wedded wife' (72), making the child legitimate, but she has mixed feelings about the man: he has abandoned her and the baby, but she evidently pities him (78). He is, rather vaguely, 'gone and far away' (80). She has sought him 'far and wide' (94) without success, yet at the end of the poem she expresses a wild hope: 'We'll find thy father in the wood' (98). Her broken train of thought in this last **stanza** suggests both mental instability and desperation. Between the lines on her husband come those about her knowing – rather ominously – 'the poisons of the shade', as well as 'the earth-nuts fit for food' (95–6). This erratic presentation of information further suggests her mental instability.

CHECK THE POEM

The erratic, unfocused speech of the mother in 'The Mad Mother' can be compared with the mental changes of direction made by the **narrator** of 'The Forsaken Indian Woman'.

The complex **metre** of the poem is set against the woman's mental disorder, containing it within a framework. It combines rhyming **couplets** with a **quatrain** mid-**stanza** and there is an internal rhyme in the penultimate line of each stanza, as in 'sung … among' (9).

GLOSSARY

54	**hollow snows** not solid, liable to give way underfoot
100	**for aye** for ever

LINES WRITTEN NEAR RICHMOND, UPON THE THAMES, AT EVENING

- The poet contemplates the River Thames and reflects on other poets.

Wordsworth contemplates the River Thames, commenting on its beauty and on its ever-changing aspect. This makes him consider the nature of life, and recall the poet William Collins, who went mad and died young. The poem falls into two distinct parts: the first sixteen lines, in later editions printed separately as 'Lines: Written when sailing in a boat at evening', and the remaining twenty-four lines, printed as 'Remembrance of Collins: Written upon the Thames near Richmond'. Wordsworth said later that the inspiration for the poem came to him while walking by the Thames, rather than being in a boat (see stanza 3, 'by thy side').

COMMENTARY

In this poem Wordsworth captures a moment of serene beauty on the River Thames and uses it to **symbolise** the progress of human life. The wave created by the boat's progress through the water reflects the summer twilight sky as the boat glides towards the sunset. Wordsworth comments on how dark the water behind the boat is by comparison, whereas a moment before the same water was lit up. The boat's silence perhaps corresponds to the way in which time passes quietly unobserved. Certainly there is a great sense of time passing, and of the transitory nature of existence.

The water before the boat is 'smiling' (6) with reflected light, yet the same water becomes the dark 'backward stream' (5) as the boat passes over it. This 'backward stream' can be seen as representing the darker times of life that inevitably follow happy times, or even as death inevitably following life. To pursue the analogy, the passing water may still reflect the evening light for someone downstream, just as our darker times may be happier times for others, and just as others will live after us. Wordsworth's **metaphor** portrays the river as a faithless lover 'beguiling' (8) those that come after him.

CHECK THE NET

Find out more about the poet William Collins (1721–59), a precursor of the **Romantics**, by searching for him on **www.litgothic.com**. His page there has a link to the full text of his 'Ode Occasioned by the Death of Mr Thomson' **alluded** to in this poem.

CHECK THE BOOK

Other authors have used the Thames as an inspiration and a symbol. Joseph Conrad (1857–1924) ends *The Heart of Darkness* with the following lines: '... the tranquil waterway leading to the uttermost ends of the earth flowed sombre under an overcast sky – seemed to lead into the heart of an immense darkness.'

CHECK THE POEM

The setting of 'Prothalamion' by Edmund Spenser (1552–99) is the Thames. He describes walking 'Along the shore of silver-streaming Thames' and in the chorus bids 'Sweet Thames run softly, till I end my song'.

CHECK THE NET

The Tate Gallery's website **www.tate. org.uk** has a number of images of paintings of the Thames by Claude Monet and James Whistler which suggest some of the light effects referred to by Wordsworth in 'Lines written near Richmond, upon the Thames, at Evening'. Search for 'Monet + Thames'.

Continuing this image of deceit, the second **stanza** pictures the youthful and self-deceiving poet caught up in the beauty of his inspiration, imagining that it will last 'to the tomb' (12).

In stanza 3 the poet addresses the Thames directly, rather fancifully wishing that everyone, or at least all poets, might be filled with its quiet soul. He immediately dismisses this wish as being in vain, yet still asks the river to flow on in the same way, to reflect the poet's nature – bright, solemn and serene. This leads him to recall the poet Collins, who at one time, at least, possessed this nature. The '*later ditty*' (30) refers to his later 'Ode occasioned by the death of Mr Thomson'. By the time he wrote this ode, Collins had become subject to depression, which he hints at in the poem. This is the 'distress' (31) to which Wordsworth refers. The 'pity' (32) is that felt by Collins for the dead Thomson.

In the final stanza, Wordsworth paraphrases a line in Collins's poem in which he offers homage to Thomson: 'And oft suspend the dashing oar'. In a later edition of *Lyrical Ballads*, the 'him' in 'For him suspend the dashing oar' (34) is printed in italics, to show that Wordsworth is recommending paying Collins the same homage that Collins paid to Thomson. Wordsworth asks the reader to pray that no other poet will experience the 'freezing sorrows' (36) felt by Collins. The last lines of the poem fulfil Wordsworth's own request in imagination, creating the peace of 'the oar suspended' (38). This conveys an image of time itself being suspended, while paradoxically the river, a symbol of passing time, flows on in silence. The phrase 'holiest powers' (40) perhaps refers to powers of nature rather than angelic powers in the conventional Christian sense, yet it clearly shows that this moment has spiritual significance for Wordsworth.

EXPOSTULATION AND REPLY

- The poet quotes a friend who asks him why he is dreaming his time away.
- The poet replies, arguing a case for quiet and receptive contemplation.

Wordsworth later claimed that this poem was based on a conversation with a friend who was overly attached to books on modern moral philosophy – called Matthew in the poem. This may in fact have been the essayist William Hazlitt. The speaker who opens the poem urges William to pursue knowledge by reading, and to stop dreaming his time away.

COMMENTARY

Wordsworth here pits the rival claims of intellectual enquiry and passively receptive contemplation of nature as paths to wisdom. The friend, 'Matthew', sees books as the sole source of knowledge. Without them, we are 'forlorn and blind' (6). He is probably thinking especially of the classics, since he refers to 'the spirit breath'd/ From dead men to their kind' (8). He jokingly accuses Wordsworth of lacking purpose, 'first-born birth' (11) probably referring to the biblical Adam. This is a little **ironic**, since Adam, before the Fall, was presumably in a state of bliss: man had no purpose until the world became imperfect, post-Eden.

Wordsworth replies with an argument in favour of allowing oneself to slip into a non-purposeful state, into being rather than doing. This is very like the attitude of mind advocated by Taoism and Buddhism, which is the opposite of that promoted by the Protestant work ethic, which encourages human beings to strive to achieve. Although Wordsworth is not specific, when he speaks of 'powers' (21), he presumably means those of nature, which impress themselves on the senses when sitting quietly by 'Esthwaite lake' (13). Wordsworth recommends listening to the voices of nature 'for ever speaking' (26) rather than chasing after knowledge intellectually.

CONTEXT

William Hazlitt (1778–1830), essayist and literary critic, was a friend and admirer of Coleridge and Wordsworth. He spent time with them in Coleridge's house in Somerset, and wrote of them 'With what eyes these poets see nature!' He shared many of their views on philosophy and literature, but was evidently more bookish than Wordsworth.

CHECK THE BOOK

Taoism was probably founded by the Chinese sage Lao-Tse (604–531BCE). The principles of Taoism, including the virtue of 'being' rather than 'doing', are described in the *Tao Te Ching* (Filiquarian Publishing, 2006).

Most of the poem is simple in tone, as befits the simplicity of mind that Wordsworth advocates, and it conveys a sense of calm resolution in its return, in the last **stanza** to the 'old grey stone' (1) of the first.

THE TABLES TURNED

- The poet urges a friend to leave his books and learn from the joys of nature instead.

This is a companion piece to 'Expostulation and Reply', although the speaker here is not necessarily Wordsworth himself. Alternatively, one could see the speaker as Wordsworth in a more vigorous mood. In this poem, there is no conversation, only the speaker urging his bookish companion to come outside and experience nature.

 CHECK THE POEM

Wordsworth's pleasure in birdsong as a natural expression of joy is echoed in Emily Brontë's 'Loud without the wind was roaring': 'For the moors, where the linnet was trilling/ Its song on the old granite stone;/ Where the lark, the wild sky-lark, was filling/ Every breast with delight like its own!'

COMMENTARY

The **metre** of this poem is similar to that of 'Expostulation and Reply' but the second and fourth lines of most **stanzas** are a syllable short, giving the whole poem a more vigorous, almost jaunty tone. The tone is set by the repetition of 'Up! up!' at the start. Everything contributes to the speaker's lively attempt to persuade the listener, appealing both to the senses and the mind. There is the mellow glow of the sun, accentuated by the rhyming of 'mellow' and 'yellow' (6, 8), the 'long green fields' (7), and the sweet singing of the linnet and thrush. The speaker is amusingly dismissive of books, the **alliteration** of 'dull and endless' (9) emphasising their dead quality compared with the liveliness of nature. To call the thrush a 'preacher' (12) is also entertaining, and perhaps carried more weight at a time when sermons were heard more often than now. Wordsworth rhymes 'strife' with 'life', thus comparing them. There is also a comparison between the darkness indoors, and the book-reader's looks that need to be cleared (1), with the 'light of things' (15) outside, which is both literal and **metaphorical**.

Wordsworth moves from an engaging portrayal of the natural world to his argument, **personifying** Nature as a teacher. Repeatedly he compares the power of nature to teach with that of the 'barren leaves' (3) of books. His claims for nature are passionate and extreme: 'One impulse from a vernal wood' (21) will teach more that is of value than all the wise men whose words are found in books put together. To Wordsworth, our 'meddling intellect' (26) interferes with the natural joy of our direct experience of beauty. The assertion 'We murder to dissect' (28) may refer literally to dissection for scientific purposes, but it also implies dissection in the sense of intellectual analysis. As in 'Expostulation and Reply', Wordsworth advocates a receptive heart as a better route to true knowledge than a striving mind. There is a slight **irony**, of course, in that anyone reading this poem is reading a book rather than out listening to thrushes and linnets.

GLOSSARY

2	**toil and trouble** hard work; a phrase taken from the Witches' spell in *Macbeth*
4	**grow double** become doubled up (or perhaps develop double vision)
13	**throstle** song-thrush
21	**vernal** spring-time
29	**science ... art** in Wordsworth's time, knowledge and its practice, not thought of as opposites at the time

OLD MAN TRAVELLING

- The poet describes an unusually patient and mild-mannered old man.
- We learn that he is going to visit his dying son in hospital.

Wordsworth told Isabella Fenwick that these lines were an overflow from 'The Old Cumberland Beggar' (1798), and they do appear to

CHECK THE POEM

The old man in 'Old Man Travelling' has a similar quiet dignity to that of another old man encountered and questioned by Wordsworth in a longer poem, 'The Leech-Gatherer'. The latter's '... words came feebly, from a feeble chest,/ But each in solemn order followed each,/ With something of a lofty utterance drest.'

be a fragment, as suggested by the indentation of the first line. Indeed, the lines seem more like the beginning of a longer poem than something self-contained. As the subtitle suggests, it is a 'sketch' rather than a completed portrait.

COMMENTARY

These lines of quiet, dignified **blank verse** match the character of the man they describe. His unobtrusive manner is such that even the birds ignore him. Everything about him is in subtle harmony. The repeated 's' sounds of 'insensibly subdued/ To settled quiet' (7–8) produce a hush that matches their sense. He has been patient for so long that now he no longer needs to exercise patience. The rolling rhythm and easy **syntax** of the lines reflect this.

In the second part of the poem, following the description of the old man, Wordsworth reports that he asked the old man where he was going, and why. The old man's response – that he is going to visit his dying son – underlines his quiet equanimity. One might expect him to be distressed at such a time, but he merely states the purpose of his journey without further comment or emotion. The violent circumstances in which the son was mortally wounded are in contrast to the old man's mild manner.

CONTEXT

In referring to a naval battle in 'Old Man Travelling', Wordsworth could be thinking of a battle with France, with whom Britain was at war between 1793 and 1802. Falmouth, on the south Cornish coast, was an important port during this war.

GLOSSARY	
subtitle	**Animal** this had two possible meanings in Wordsworth's day: (1) relating to mental and nervous function; (2) to do with physical energy. The old man seems to be both physically and mentally calm
19	**Falmouth** a small port on the south Cornish coast where British naval ships might return from fighting the French in the Channel

THE COMPLAINT OF A FORSAKEN INDIAN WOMAN

- A sick Native American woman has been abandoned by her tribe.
- She prays for death, and then blames herself, then her tribe, for her plight.
- She laments that her baby has been given to another woman.
- She says she will follow her companions, but then resigns herself to death.

This is an unusual poem in the collection: a quietly moving first-person lament in the voice of a woman from a culture with which Wordsworth was only familiar through reading. Though the woman's outlook is generally stoical, she does go through a number of changes of outlook during the course of the poem. This perhaps reflects the fact that she is sick, hungry and perhaps beginning to freeze to death. In particular, she laments the loss of her baby son. The poem is in an eighteenth-century genre in which individuals from exotic cultures address the reader at the point of death or in some other crisis situation. Wordsworth's is not the only 'dying Indian' poem.

COMMENTARY

The first-person **narrative** is a strong feature of the poem. The woman tells her story cursorily, revealing only that she has been abandoned by her companions because she was too weak and sick to continue on their journey. Her baby son has been given to another woman, and she now faces death. Her fire has died out, her water is frozen over, and her food has been stolen by a wolf. She is now too weak to follow her tribe, although for a moment, in the penultimate **stanza**, she says that she will do so. Rather than relating in any detail what has led up to this moment, the poem focuses on the woman's shifting thoughts and feelings as she composes herself to face death.

CHECK THE POEM

A more recent poem about a Native American woman abandoned by her tribe is 'The Forsaken' by Duncan Campbell-Scott (1862–1947). A more famous poem featuring Native Americans is *The Song of Hiawatha*, by H. W. Longfellow (1807–82).

CONTEXT

At the end of the eighteenth century, educated people in Britain had some awareness of Native Americans, especially as many eastern tribes had fought in the American War of Independence – mostly on the British side.

CONTEXT

The Northern Lights (*Aurora Borealis*) are moving, coloured lights which occur in the sky at northern latitudes when charged particles from the magnetosphere collide with atoms and molecules from the upper atmosphere. They have a spiritual and mythical significance for Native American tribes.

The opening stanza begins and ends with the woman praying that her body will 'die away', perhaps implying that her soul will survive – although she says nothing explicit about an afterlife. Her sleeping vision of the Northern Lights seems to be one of foreboding, since it is a rare occurrence and was probably attended by superstitions or beliefs. At the very least, it imbues this moment in time with a special significance, as if the sky itself is saluting the dying woman. The description of the phenomenon, which she perceives only in her sleep, blurs the distinction between the woman's inner state and the outer world. The short line 'And yet I am alive' (8) is arresting – as if she expected the Northern Lights to herald her imminent death. The stanza also contains several references to sight, suggestive of inner and outer vision.

Stanza 2 focuses on the woman's fire, which is now dead. This probably means she will freeze to death, but the fire also symbolises her desire to live. The bald phrase 'and I remain' (12) underlines the incongruity of her physically outliving her desire to live. She briefly remembers life's simple pleasures before renouncing them. Even so, it is surprising to hear that she is now 'contented' (19) to die. This contentment is immediately undermined in the next stanza, when she blames her tribe for not dragging her on with them for longer, and then switches to blaming herself for succumbing to despair. Strangely, it is this despair, it seems, that prevented her from following her tribe even when she lay 'strong and without pain' for a while (29).

The woman's grief is strongest when she recalls her child. Elsewhere the very regular iambic metre reflects the narrator's stoicism, but in lines 31–2 this is broken by the addition of an unstressed syllable at the end of each line, creating a feminine rhyme. The picture of the baby being strangely moved, 'As if he strove to be a man' (37) is touching. It also reveals what the woman omits from her narrative – the fact that she has no husband. The next stanza continues to express her grief over her child, suggesting that she died when parted from him. However, she still longs to send a message on the wind to her departed companions. She has already mentioned the fire, earth (ashes) and water. This mention of the wind (air) completes the round of the four elements, to which she will return physically in death. (Water appears as ice in line 13 and again in line 56.)

The narrator's confusion is apparent when she momentarily resolves to follow her companions (51–4), before returning again to thoughts of death. The wolf is a **symbolic** harbinger of death, as well as helping to ensure it by stealing her food. It is a cold comfort to her that she is alone, and therefore may as well die (59–60). The fact that the wolf has come 'to-night' reminds us that the poem is being narrated at night: the woman will literally 'not see another sun' (62). By the last stanza she is either too weak or too cold to lift her limbs. Almost her last thoughts are of her lost child. Although on the conscious level she is longing to see him, the use of the word 'happy' in lines 67 and 68 raise the mood of the poem so that it does not end on an entirely miserable note. The last two lines are almost a repeat of those which open and close the first stanza. However, they reverse the order of the lines and change the wording slightly. Before, she prayed that she would not see another day; now she *feels* her body 'die away' and is certain that her prayer has been answered: 'I shall not see another day' (69–70).

> **CONTEXT**
>
> The Four Elements – fire, earth, air and water – play an important role in Native American cosmology, as for many other cultural groups worldwide.

GLOSSARY

24	**heartless** dispirited, disheartened

THE CONVICT

- The poet turns reluctantly from nature to visit a prisoner.
- He describes the prison's appalling conditions, sympathising with the prisoner.

CHECK THE NET

Find information on the early history of prison reform and the reform work of John Howard (1726–90), by searching for his name on **www.bbc.co.uk**

Written in 1796, at a time of great public debate on the penal system, Wordsworth's poem can be seen alongside Coleridge's 'The Dungeon' in its criticism of prison conditions and their effect. However, whereas 'The Dungeon' presents an intellectual argument against prisons, 'The Convict' works more through the emotional appeal of a **gothic romance** description of an individual convict and his sufferings. On another level it can be seen as an **allegory** of the human being's imprisonment in mortality.

COMMENTARY

Whereas Coleridge's 'The Dungeon' moves from discussion of prison conditions to nature as an alternative, 'The Convict' begins with the poet reluctantly turning from the joys of nature, that 'dwelling so fair' (5), to visit a convict. We leave the healthy and positive 'glory of evening' and the 'calm season of rest' in **stanza** 1 for the 'thick-ribbed walls' of the prison (9), the phrase itself suggesting human confinement within the body. Here there is little light: the convict is seen through 'the glimmering grate' (11), though this also hints at the faint hope created by the poet's visit.

CONTEXT

To the **Romantics**, prisons were associated with oppression. The fall of the Bastille, the notorious Paris prison, on 14 July 1789, was hailed by those opposed to the Establishment as a blow against despotism. Wordsworth took part in the anniversary celebrations in 1790.

Unlike many of the **ballads** in the collection, the convict is unnamed, as if his identity has been taken away. In its place is an image of suffering humanity, despair and dejection. He is described in gothic terms: his 'black-matted head' (13), deep sighing, and intent gaze on 'the fetters that link him to death' (16). This last phrase perhaps points to the likelihood that he will die in prison, but on the allegorical level it also marks him as a representative of all humanity, fettered to a mortal body. However, stanzas 5 and 6 tell us that even worse than these physical privations are the torments of guilt which the convict suffers. Even this emotional pain is couched in intense physical **imagery**:

His bones are consumed, and his life-blood is dried,
    With wishes the past to undo. (21–2)

It is as if the man's conscience is eating away at his very body.

Stanza 7 rather incongruously takes us away from contemplation of
the convict to compare his lot with that of the monarch. Perhaps
Wordsworth's anti-monarchical and anti-clerical sympathies are
revealed here. Ostensibly he is simply saying that when a king
leaves the Church council ('synod', 25) or the battlefield, he is
pampered and can recover himself through sleep. However, the
description of the synod as 'dark' and the epithet 'blood-reeking'
(25) are negatives which perhaps detract from the main focus of the
poem. Wordsworth's point is that the convict has no 'soothers of
sense' to help him escape his grief in sleep; rather, he must try to
sleep amidst 'uproar' and, moreover, in 'the comfortless vault of
disease' (31–2). The terrible sense of confinement is reinforced by
the fetters pressing on him (33) and by the fact that if he so much as
turns in his 'half-slumber', the noise of his chains sets the jail-
mastiff howling, which in turn throws the poor man into a sweat of
terror. The 'thousand sharp punctures' (39) are evocative, if a little
melodramatic.

The poet's reintroduction of himself in the final two stanzas is
problematic. He presents himself, as if addressing the convict, as a
well-wisher 'come as a brother thy sorrows to share' (48). However,
he patently cannot share the man's sorrows, although he is
sympathetic. Moreover, it is hard not to see his identifying himself
as one 'whose first wish is the wish to be good' (47) as comparing
himself favourably with the convict. The final stanza is also rather
awkward, with its slightly convoluted **personifications** of
compassion and virtue. Wordsworth is essentially saying that even if
compassion changes her nature on hearing the convict's name, and
even if his reputation is a slur in the 'proud mouth' (50) of Virtue,
he (Wordsworth) would, if he could, remove the man from prison
and place him where he might become a better man. The final
image, of the poet planting the man where he might 'blossom' (52),
like a flower, points to Wordsworth's belief in the rehabilitating and
restorative power of nature.

CONTEXT

In reality an
English king at the
end of the
eighteenth
century would be
unlikely to go
anywhere near a
battlefield, so
Wordsworth's
reference to the
'blood-reeking
field' (25) is rather
fanciful.

CHECK THE POEM

A famous example of a poem with an anapaestic metre is 'The Destruction of Sennacherib' by Lord Byron (1788–1824). It begins: 'The Assyrian came down like a wolf on the fold/ And his cohorts were gleaming in purple and gold.'

While the **anapaestic metre** of the poem and its regular *abab* rhyme scheme were not unusual in protest poems of the time, to the modern ear they undermine its serious intent. Indeed they have been used in many music hall songs. Employed here, they lack the gravity of **blank verse,** which Coleridge uses so effectively in 'The Dungeon'. Nonetheless, the use of **enjambment,** for example in stanza 10, helps to prevent the metre from becoming overly dominant.

GLOSSARY	
3	**calm season of rest** night-time; Wordsworth refers to the birdsong that comes before nightfall
25	**field** battlefield
37	**mastiff** a type of large guard dog
52	**plant** establish, as well as plant in the horticultural sense

EXTENDED COMMENTARIES

THE RIME OF THE ANCYENT MARINERE, PART IV

The opening of this section focuses on the person of the Ancient Mariner himself, and on his possibly supernatural nature, already suggested by his 'glittering eye' and his ability to reduce the wedding guest to childlike obedience (Part I, stanza 5). The old man's physical appearance is threatening in a number of ways. His twice-mentioned 'skinny hand' (217, 221) and his dark colouring recall the skeletal figure of Death in Part III. Less literally, his likeness to 'the ribb'd Sea-sand' (219) recalls both Death and the 'naked ribs' (177) of the hulk in which he and his female companion travel. His tanned skin is that of someone sufficiently low down the social scale to spend a lot of time outdoors, which in itself would pose some degree of threat to Coleridge's middle- and upper-class readership, especially with Britain being at war with Revolutionary France. However, it is the thought that he might be a ghost that most alarms the wedding guest, judging by the reassurance that the Ancient Mariner feels he has to give him.

Ironically, the fact that he did not die with his shipmates is what condemns the Ancient Mariner to his appalling solitude. He uses the word 'alone' four times in **stanza 3**. He thinks he has been abandoned even by Christ, and for company has only 'a million, million slimy things' (23), the vagueness of the phrase somehow contributing to the sense of primeval horror. Even the sea itself, often regarded as a source of life, is said to be 'rotting' (232). For the Ancient Mariner there is no relief wherever he looks, and his efforts at prayer are thwarted by his own 'wicked whisper' (238), stemming either from the devil or from his own resentment at his plight. His spiritual thirst is reflected in this whisper making his 'heart as dry as dust' (239). A strong sense of the pressure to which he feels subjected is contained in the image of his pulsing eyeballs, and in the following long, rhythmically arresting **couplet**:

> For the sky and the sea, and the sea and the sky
> Lay like a load on my weary eye. (242–3)

CONTEXT

At the time when *The Rime of the Ancyent Marinere* is set, an old sailor might well have been regarded with a mixture of interest and suspicion. Sailors were well known for tall tales of outlandish creatures and tribes they claimed to have encountered in far-off lands. Shakespeare's *The Tempest* could be seen as one such tall tale.

CHECK THE POEM

Many poets have used the sea as a symbol of infinity or immortality. For example, Shelley (1792–1822), in 'Unfathomable Sea' writes: 'Thou shoreless flood, which in thy ebb and flow/ Claspest the limits of mortality!'

THE RIME OF THE ANCYENT MARINERE, PART IV continued

The inverted repetition of words in the first line (sky ... sea, sea ... sky) suggests the way in which the unnaturally calm sea presents a mirror image of the sky. Their combined weight on the Ancient Mariner's vision is emphasised by the **alliteration** in the second line, and in the rhyme. This second line also stands out because it is an addition to the normal **quatrain**.

Turning his eyes from sea and sky, the Ancient Mariner sees only the dead men, whose bodies seem to be supernaturally preserved from putrefaction, and whose eyes still hold the curse they lay on him in the moment of their death. Another long **stanza** (stanza 9) emphasises the horror of this curse and how it has remained with the Ancient Mariner.

The soft passage of the moon, accompanied by stars, is in peaceful contrast to the plight of the Ancient Mariner, and to the burning (probably phosphorescent) sea in the ship's shadow. This paves the way for the Ancient Mariner's important sighting of the water-snakes (264–73), 'shining white' in the moonlight, but richly coloured in the ship's shadow. This is the point at which he begins to become more positive in his outlook. The water-snakes which he now joyously greets – 'O happy living things' (274) are those same 'slimy things' that populated a 'rotting Sea' in lines 230–2. It is the mariner's new vision of life that makes 'A spring of love' gush from his heart (276), so that he is moved, unthinkingly, to bless these beautiful creatures. The image of the spring is in contrast to the thirst, literal and spiritual, felt earlier by the Ancient Mariner and other crew members.

The significance of the line 'And I blessed them unaware!' (277) is emphasised by its exact repetition at the end of the stanza. It is this softening of the Ancient Mariner's heart towards other living creatures, in contrast to his shooting of the albatross, which frees his spirit so that he can pray. He is returned to the communion of souls, as shown **symbolically** by his release from the albatross, originally hung about his neck by his shipmates, and therefore symbolising their curse. The homely but effective **simile** describing its sinking 'like lead into the sea' (283) emphasises the great weight of the spiritual oppression from which he has been freed. His ability to

CHECK THE BOOK

Marine phosphorescence was a phenomenon described by sailors and travel writers in Coleridge's time. Caused by plankton giving off light, especially when the sea is disturbed, it features in William Golding's *Lord of the Flies* (1954) when Simon's body is washed out to sea.

pray signifies his readmission to Christian grace, even if Part VI
reveals that he still has more penance to do.

GLOSSARY

219	ribb'd Sea-sand undulating, like ribs, from the action of waves
234	eldritch ghastly, eerie
259	bemock'd the sultry main mocked the oppressively hot sea, perhaps because the moonlight produces the appearance of coolness without giving any actual relief
262	chalmed becalmed, motionless
268	hoary white, like flakes of frost

THE THORN

In this strange and controversial poem Wordsworth emulates the
tradition of the folk **ballad** yet develops it in his own way. It can be
compared with 'The Idiot Boy' in this respect, and in its focus on
motherhood. In 'The Idiot Boy', however, the mother is wholly
adoring of her son and is happily reunited with him, whereas in 'The
Thorn' the mother has either lost or murdered her baby, and is left in
a state of seemingly unremitting misery as a result. Another similarity
between the two is the way in which Wordsworth uses his role as
narrator. In 'The Idiot Boy' he speaks more or less as himself, but in
'The Thorn' there is a more developed **persona**. However, both
narrators pretend to have only partial knowledge of the story they
tell. In 'The Thorn', this is developed into a study of small-
community gossip, rumour and suspicion. Much of what we are told
consists of critical speculation, passed on rather disingenuously by
the narrator, and we are in the end left to make up our own minds
about whether or not Martha Ray has murdered her baby.

Metrically the poem is more ambitious than 'The Idiot Boy',
consisting of eleven-line stanzas which combine **blank** and rhymed
verse. There are two short lines in each stanza, which convey a sense
of something cut short – perhaps like the baby's life – and which force
us to pause, as if echoing the narrator's uncertainty. There are also a
number of **end-stopped** rhyming lines that give the poem a folk-

CONTEXT

Wordsworth said
of 'The Thorn':
'Arose out of my
observing, on the
ridge of Quantock
Hills, on a stormy
day, a thorn which
I had often passed
in calm and bright
weather without
noticing it. I said
to myself, "Cannot
I by some
invention do as
much to make this
Thorn
permanently an
impressive object
as the storm has
made it to my eyes
at this moment?"'
(Note by Isabella
Fenwick, 1843).

The Thorn continued

CONTEXT

A number of
English folksongs
survive which tell
the story of young
women courted
and jilted by their
lovers; for example
'The Blacksmith'.

**CHECK
THE BOOK**

J. K. Stephen
(1859–92) **parodied**
Wordsworth's
sonnet 'Thoughts of
a Briton on the
Subjugation of
Switzerland', saying
that Wordsworth
had 'two voices ...
one is of the deep ...
And one is of an old
half-witted sheep/
Which bleats
articulate
monotony,/ And
indicates that two
and one are three,/
That grass is green,
lakes damp, and
mountains steep.'

ballad feel but which can seem heavy-handed at times, as in the infamous rhyming **couplet** at the end of **stanza** III. The **diction**, too, is conversational and suited to a ballad, and even the rare **similes** are unsophisticated, as in 'the stormy winter gale/ Cuts like a scythe'.

The poem is a combination of ghost story and murder mystery, though it also includes the folk tradition theme of the jilted lover. Martha Ray has been 'blithe and gay' (stanza XI) thinking of Stephen Hill. The fact that she gave him her company 'with a maiden's true good will' suggests that she also gave him her maidenhead – as implied by the scarlet cloak (stanza VI), denoting a 'fallen woman', that she still wears twenty-two years later.

Although Martha Ray is the central character of the poem, Wordsworth takes great care to set the scene over the course of the first five stanzas before we even encounter her. At the **symbolic** centre of the poem is the thorn tree itself. It grows 'High on a mountain's highest ridge' (stanza III), exposed to the elements. Described as stunted, 'old and grey', leafless, 'a mass of knotted joints', 'A wretched thing forlorn' (stanza I) and hung with lichen and mosses which appear intent on dragging it to the ground (stanza II), it at least in part represents the state of Martha Ray herself. Indeed she, too, is described as 'wretched' in stanza VII. The tree is even associated with a child (stanza I) well before we learn of the rumours attached to it.

The second symbolic element of the poem is the 'little muddy Pond' introduced in stanza II. The banality of the description here, and especially the measurements locating the pond and giving its exact size – 'three feet long and two feet wide' – have often been ridiculed by critics. However, this probably represents Wordsworth's attempt to ground the description in reality. The narrator wants to emphasise that he has seen these things with his own eyes: they are verifiable, unlike the rumours attached to them.

Wordsworth also introduces the poem's third symbol, the mossy hillock, well before we meet Martha Ray, devoting two whole stanzas to it. In contrast with the decrepit thorn tree, the mossy hillock is 'a fresh and lovely sight' (IV). Whereas the tree is grey and leafless, the hillock is resplendent with colour. Wordsworth breaks the general tone of the poem, and even the whole collection, with the courtly and conventionally poetic image of the 'mossy network' seemingly woven 'by hand of lady fair' (IV). The 'cups' are blossoms, but with the added suggestion of cupping blood in the medical sense, a sense reinforced by their blood-red colour.

It is a feature of the poem that the story proceeds by hints. Thus the hillock is at first described simply as being 'like an infant's grave in size', rather than actually being one (stanza V). This technique echoes the veiled hints of rumour-mongers, as well as helping to develop the sinister tone of a ghost story. The latter is also added to by the overlapping use of language. Having described the tree, pond and hillock, Wordsworth reiterates in stanza VI:

> Now would you see this aged thorn,
> This pond and beauteous hill of moss …

In stanza IX we read:

> The heap that's like an infant's grave,
> The pond – and thorn, so old and grey …

In stanza XX the three symbols are again listed, this time in the voice of the **narrator**'s imaginary interlocutor, and with the addition of 'the creeping breeze' that stirs the little pond. The effect of this technique of overlapping is to add more and more implied significance to the objects mentioned, so that they become increasingly sinister.

There are further hints of the sinister in the description of Martha Ray herself. The narrator advises us to 'take care' to choose our time to cross the mountain to see the spot, in order to avoid the woman sitting '… between the heap/ That's like an infant's grave in size,/ And that same pond of which I spoke'. She is 'wretched' (stanza VII), a 'poor woman' (stanza VIII), 'this unhappy woman' (stanza X), yet the narrator tells us that no one dare 'Approach the spot when she is there' (stanza IX).

Wordsworth engages us further in the unravelling of Martha Ray's tale by introducing in stanza X the unnamed questioner, to whom

> **CONTEXT**
>
> In an era before contraceptives, abortion and the welfare state, when unmarried mothers were shunned as 'fallen women', the killing of a newborn baby by its mother would have been a tragically familiar story.

The Thorn continued

the **narrator** characteristically professes to have only partial knowledge (as in 'The Idiot Boy'). He promises to do his best to inform the questioner before he goes up the mountain. He becomes notably involved with Martha Ray's plight in **stanza XIII**:

> Oh me! ten thousand times I'd rather
> That he had died, that cruel father!

We see the influence of the folk story again in XIV, with the verdict of Old Farmer Simpson. Immediately after this, however, the narrator retreats to the tone of someone who is prepared to pass on rumours but will not be held responsible for their accuracy. All he will vouch for is that the old woman does visit the thorn tree in her scarlet cloak. He reveals this in stanzas XVII–XIX, in which his personal anecdote brings the poem to a climax. He describes how he climbed the mountain with his telescope – another mundane detail with which Wordsworth attempts to give the story credibility – and at the height of a driving storm mistook the woman for 'a jutting crag'. His line 'Her face it was enough for me' tantalisingly fails to reveal exactly what he saw, but we assume that it was shocking, or even frightening.

Stanzas XX–XXII return to local rumour. After more questions, it comes as a sudden shock to hear that '… some will say/ She hanged her baby on the tree' or 'drowned it in the pond'. The further rumour that the 'scarlet moss is red/ With drops of that poor infant's blood' creates a vividly persuasive mental image, so that when the narrator denies that the mother could 'kill a new-born infant thus' we cannot be sure if this is sincere or **ironic**. Perhaps Wordsworth wants to keep us guessing. The details of the infant's face in the pond (stanza XXI) and the shaking earth (stanza XXII) are in the tradition of the **gothic** ghost story, but in the end the narrator leaves us only with the certainty that an inconsolably lamenting woman does visit the scene of the supposed crime.

CONTEXT

Mary Magdalene is a biblical figure first mentioned in Luke 8:1–3. She has traditionally been regarded as a former prostitute and as such is depicted in paintings wearing red.

 QUESTION

Do you think Wordsworth intends us to believe that Martha Ray killed her baby, or that the rumours are false – or are we meant to be left uncertain?

GLOSSARY

| 40 | **net-work** a form of needlework |
| 43 | **cups** blossoms, but also suggesting medical blood-letting |

THE IDIOT BOY

This is a **narrative** poem in which Wordsworth is present as an imperfect **narrator**, pretending to have only partial knowledge of the story – and none at all of what befalls the 'idiot boy' during his nine-hour absence when sent by his mother to fetch the doctor for a sick neighbour. One feature of the poem is its handling of pace in the gradual rise of Betty's anxiety when her son fails to return. Another is the contrast between speculation about the boy's fate, and our actual ignorance of it at the end of the poem.

The poem is a study of a mother's non-judgemental love for her son, and of the mystery of his joyful experience of the world – and especially of nature. There is ample evidence that Betty adores her son. He is 'Him whom you love' (11) and 'Him whom she loves' (15, 51), her 'best delight' (63). She is almost more concerned that he will simply return (70) than that he will bring the doctor for Susan. When Betty sees him on their pony ready to leave, her 'face with joy o'erflows' (98). She is 'Proud of herself, and proud of him' (99), despite his lack of conventional understanding. She is, as it turns out, over-optimistic about his ability to carry out his errand of mercy. Wordsworth himself comments, addressing himself directly to Betty:

> There's not a mother, no not one,
> But when she hears what you have done,
> O Betty, she'll be in a fright. (24–6)

Even as he sets off, he seems to have already lost any sense of the practical purpose of his journey:

> For joy he cannot hold the bridle,
> For joy his head and heels are idle,
> He's idle all for very joy. (84–6)

The repetition of the word 'joy' here emphasises Johnny's principal characteristic, and the one which endears him to Wordsworth. Such is his intense happiness that he forgets 'his holly whip/ And all his skill in horsemanship' (94–5). He is 'happy, happy, happy John' (96).

CHECK THE FILM

John Mills won an Oscar for his role as the 'village idiot' in the film *Ryan's Daughter* (dir. David Lean, 1970).

CHECK THE BOOK

The main character in Fyodor Dostoevsky's novel *The Idiot* (1868) is Prince Myshkin, who is in a sense 'an idiot', or at least an innocent, in that he sees only good in people, and lacks all understanding of falsehood and contrivance.

CHECK THE POEM

The moon is the inspiration of Philip Larkin's poem 'Sad Steps' in *High Windows* (1974). He calls it a 'Lozenge of love' and a 'Medallion of art'.

CONTEXT

The owl has been associated with wisdom since the time of the ancient Greeks. Wordsworth's association of owls with Johnny may hint at him having a kind of wisdom.

Johnny is also linked several times to the moon under which he travels, the moon being traditionally associated with madness and mental deficiency – as in the word *lunacy* – but also with inspiration. For example:

> The moon that shines above his head
> Is not more still and mute than he. (90–1)

Although Johnny loves to make an unintelligible 'burring' sound, the muteness ascribed to him is another significant feature, along with his stillness:

> The silence of her Idiot Boy,
> What hope it sends to Betty's heart! (105–6)

His quietness and stillness set him apart from the bustle and chatter of ordinary humanity, including that of his own mother. Thus his intellectual deficiency seems to enable him to enjoy the universe purely and intensely without the distractions experienced by the conventional mind. In fact, he is identified more closely with nature, and with the animal world in particular, than with the world of civilised humanity. His 'burring' seems to be in harmony with the hooting of the owls – mentioned several times in the poem:

> And Johnny's in a merry tune,
> The owlets hoot, the owlets curr,
> And Johnny's lips they burr, burr, burr,
> And on he goes beneath the moon. (113–16)

The next **stanza** identifies him even more explicitly with the horse on which he rides: 'His steed and he right well agree' (117) in their placid good humour. When we last see the pair in the first part of the poem, they are combined in their mission: 'So through the moonlight lanes they go' (127), as if horse and boy are equally responsible for fetching the doctor.

While we hear nothing about what actually befalls the boy during the night – other than his enigmatic lines at the end of the poem (460–1) – there is a great deal of speculation, first from his mother

(224–41), then from Wordsworth as **narrator** (327–47). Betty imagines him leaving his horse to 'hunt the moon that's in the brook' (225), climbing into an oak tree and staying there (234), being persuaded to go away with gypsies (236), carried off into 'the goblin's hall', lost in the castle among ghosts (240) or 'playing with the waterfall' (241). These thoughts say as much about the boy's association with nature, wildness and mystery as they do about a mother's tendency to fear the worst.

Wordsworth as narrator imagines more literary possibilities, though they also echo folk stories. The boy could be trying to catch a star, riding back to front on his horse, hunting sheep, or riding on for ever like the devil on horseback. Wordsworth's rather jocular tone here – especially the gently **ironic** description of the boy as 'A fierce and dreadful hunter' (338) – reassures us that the boy is actually unharmed. At the same time these ideas identify the boy with the archetype of the Holy Fool, who approaches the world innocently, and who has a kind of wisdom in seeing it differently from others. The same idea is echoed in the boy's only comments on his night-ride, in which he sees the owls as cockerels and the moon as a cold sun (460–1).

Wordsworth's position as narrator is of special interest in this poem. At times he addresses Betty, pretending ignorance of her purpose – for example, in stanzas 1, 4 and 5. This ploy is taken to an extreme in his speculations about Johnny's fate, which lead him to address the Muses, begging them to let him tell 'But half of what to him befell' (350), and reproaching them for denying him this knowledge. This provides a **narrative** justification for leaving Johnny's actual experience a mystery. Even more striking is the way in which Wordsworth positions himself when the boy is finally spotted. It is as if the narrator is there in the wood, but uncertain of what he sees. He asks 'Who's yon… ?' (357) and then 'Where is she, where is Betty Foy?' (368), as if engaging the interest of a child in a bedtime story.

Stylistically the poem owes much to the **ballad** tradition. It is in rhymed **iambic quadrameter**, like many ballads, but it is unusual in having five lines in a stanza, whereas ballads almost always have four. The poem also breaks with convention by making the first line

> **CONTEXT**
>
> The idea of Johnny hunting 'the moon that's in the brook' (225) may relate to the Wiltshire 'moonrakers'. According to legend, a customs officer found two men apparently trying to fish the moon's reflection out of a pond. They claimed that they were raking in a cheese. In fact they were retrieving a smuggled barrel of brandy.

> **CONTEXT**
>
> In Greek myth, the Muses were goddesses who ruled the arts and sciences. They were thought to inspire artists, especially poets and musicians. They were the daughters of Zeus and Mnemosyne, goddess of memory.

THE IDIOT BOY continued

CONTEXT

The idea of mystical experience enabling one to 'hear the grass grow', as in line 295 of 'The Idiot Boy', was revived in the 1967 hit song 'I can hear the grass grow', by the Move.

of each **stanza** an unrhymed addition to the *abba* **quatrain**. The language is mostly quite commonplace, and there is much deliberate repetition of words and phrases. See, for example, stanza 2, and the repeated line 'Poor Susan moans, poor Susan groans' (151, 157). Some words are colloquial: 'girt', 'fiddle-faddle' (14), 'hurly-burly' (60), 'curr' (114) and 'hobnob' (299). The use of the present tense in much of the poem also echoes many ballads, as does the use of dialogue. Similarly, there is little **imagery**, and when an image does occur it is commonplace and conversational, as in Johnny's lips 'burring' 'As loud as any mill' and the pony's moving 'Meek as a lamb' (109–10). Slightly less commonplace is the line describing Betty on finding her son safe: 'She darts, as with a torrent's force' (384). This **simile** identifies her with the 'roaring waterfall' of line 370, thus emphasising the strength of her maternal feeling and associating it with the power of nature. Also in contrast with the triteness of much of the language are occasional lines of simple beauty which hint at the mystical experience of the 'idiot boy':

> The streams with softest sounds are flowing,
> The grass you almost hear it growing,
> You hear it now if e'er you can.
>
> The owlets through the long blue night
> Are shouting to each other still.
>   (294–8)

GLOSSARY

14	**girt** saddle girth (attaches the saddle)
14	**fiddle-faddle** fuss
18	**burr** make an unintelligible sound
60	**hurly-burly** loud noise combined with violent movement
139	**porringer** a small dish for gruel or porridge
209	**hies** goes
247	**distemper** unhappy mood
250	**cattle** horses
348	**indentures** a contract between an apprentice and his master

LINES WRITTEN A FEW MILES ABOVE TINTERN ABBEY

This poem is justifiably regarded as one of Wordsworth's finest, and is one of his best known. It expresses his profound thoughts and impressions relating to nature and its influence, as well as his love for his sister Dorothy who accompanied him on his return visit to the Wye Valley in 1798. It is far from being a **ballad**, and its language is more sophisticated than that found in much of the collection. Yet while being eloquent it is never unnecessarily complex; nor does it stray into any of the conventionally high-blown, self-consciously poetic **diction** of the Augustans. Its use of imagery is sparing, but in its few instances striking, as when Wordsworth refers to the 'still, sad music of humanity' (92). The use of **blank verse** helps to give the poem a suitable dignity, as does its structure. While focusing on a single subject and drawing out a range of connected reflections on it, it can be divided up into a number of parts reflecting its subtle shifts of direction. In this it can be called an **ode**, a classical form which dealt with elevated and meditative themes.

The title is something of a **conceit**: Wordsworth actually wrote the poem on returning home rather than in the Wye Valley, where Tintern Abbey is situated – although he later said that he composed it in his head over a period of a few days spent rambling in the area. The area, even then, was popular with tourists, including poets and artists. Its steep wooded slopes, winding river, cliffs, and of course the picturesque ruins of the abbey itself, were a source of inspiration for many. However, Wordsworth writes more about the effect of nature on him and Dorothy than about the valley itself. True, the first stanza goes into some detail, evoking the 'sweet inland murmur' of the Wye (4) and painting a picture of the majestic scenery: '… steep and lofty cliffs … a wild secluded scene' (5–6); the 'dark sycamore' (10) under which he imagines himself; the 'plots of cottage-ground' (11); the 'hedge-rows, little lines/ Of sportive wood run wild' (16–17). This is enough to draw us into the scene and sympathise with the effect it has on him.

After this, however, Wordsworth focuses largely on his own responses to nature, though with the addition of Dorothy's

> **CONTEXT**
>
> Although the Wye Valley in the area of Tintern Abbey was reportedly beautiful in 1798, there was a certain amount of small-scale industry. The smoke which Wordsworth describes emerging from the woods was not from the fires of vagrants or dwellers, but from charcoal burners.

 **CHECK THE POEM**

John Keats (1795–1821) wrote a number of famous odes, including 'Ode on a Grecian Urn', which begins, 'Thou still unravish'd bride of quietness,/ Thou foster-child of silence and slow time'.

LINES WRITTEN A FEW MILES ABOVE TINTERN ABBEY continued

CHECK THE BOOK

William Gilpin's *Observations on the River Wye* (1782), has been called the work that launched English tourism. Gilpin's Romantic aesthetics would be controversial now: he recommended that more of Tintern Abbey should be demolished to make it more picturesque.

CHECK THE POEM

The kind of vision described in lines 48–9 may be compared with William Blake's 'Auguries of Innocence': 'To see a world in a grain of sand,/ And a heaven in a wild flower,/ Hold infinity in the palm of your hand,/ And eternity in an hour.'

responses, and of his feelings for her. This is very much in the **Romantic** mode, but is particularly introspective even for the Romantics. Wordsworth, then, is unashamedly inviting us to view in depth the feelings and perceptions that nature generates in him, rather than revealing them as a by-product of his description of nature. He is perhaps especially conscious of his feelings because revisiting the valley after an absence of five years makes him aware of how he has changed in that time. First, though, he dwells on how, even before his return, his memories of the Wye Valley have influenced him. He is grateful that 'in lonely rooms, and mid the din/ Of towns and cities' (26–7) his memories have been restorative to him. He describes the process in some detail: 'sensations sweet,/ Felt in the blood, and felt along the heart,/ And passing even into my purer mind' (28–30). The emphasis here is very much on feeling rather than thought.

Wordsworth goes on to speculate that these memories have made him a kinder and more loving man, echoing the idea expressed elsewhere in *Lyrical Ballads* (for example, that nature has a beneficial effect on individual morality, by bringing the individual into harmony with the universe, predisposing him to 'little, nameless, unremembered acts/ Of kindness and of love' (35–6). The simple wording is touchingly modest and unassuming. More than this, he says, these memories have led him to experience the sublime, to feel 'the power/ Of harmony, and the deep power of joy', enabling him to 'see into the life of things' (48–9). Again, the description of the mystical experience is considered and detailed, yet the language is simple and understated. It is also worth noting that he does not claim to be unique in his insight, his use of 'us' and 'we' taking for granted that others also have this experience.

In the third **stanza** the poet breaks away from contemplating the nature of his mystical experience, returning initially to a more general expression of the consolation he has often felt in remembering the Wye. Bringing himself briefly back to the present, he immediately shifts into the future, anticipating the joys he will experience in years to come as he remembers the beauties of the Wye Valley: 'in this moment there is life and food/ For future years' (65–6). However, this throws him back into a very telling recollection of his former self as he was on first visiting the Wye Valley. Then, five years earlier, his response to nature was entirely emotional. Although he claims that even in this earlier time the 'coarser pleasures' of his 'boyish days' and 'their glad animal movements' (74–5) were a thing of the past, there is still something animalistic in his description of himself bounding over the mountains 'like a roe [deer]' (68). Moreover, the description of nature here borders on the melodramatic, and the feelings described are ambivalent, as if the young Wordsworth was somehow possessed by nature:

> The sounding cataract
> Haunted me like a passion: the tall rock,
> The mountain, and the deep and gloomy wood.
> (77–9)

The words 'Haunted' and 'gloomy' express something more complex than a simple love of nature. And with the wisdom of maturity, he admits to having been, in a sense, driven to lose himself in nature:

> ... more like a man
> Flying from something that he dreads, than one
> Who sought the thing he loved.   (71–3)

He experienced 'aching joys' and 'dizzy raptures' (86–7), which, again, sound romantically exciting but not sustainable, and even partly negative. What he has gained in five years, he says, is the ability to link his experience of nature to an awareness of 'The still, sad music of humanity' (92) and to look on nature more thoughtfully. He now experiences 'the joy/ Of elevated thoughts' (95–6). Yet he is not describing a merely intellectual experience: rather, he is saying that nature now moves him to an experience of the divine in all things. This is 'A motion and a spirit' (101), 'deeply interfused' (97) with all things. He falls short of naming God, but this spirit has its 'dwelling' in all nature, 'and in the mind of man' (98–100), and it has power: it 'impels/ All thinking things' (101–2). This, he explains, is why he still loves nature – despite not being possessed by it in the manner of his earlier self, and sees it as his nurse, guide, guardian and the core of his 'moral being' (112).

 CHECK THE BOOK

The 'sublime', especially as found in wild, awe-inspiring landscape, is an important Romantic concept. For an early investigation of this idea, see Edmund Burke's *Philosophical Inquiry into the Origin of our Ideas of the Sublime and the Beautiful* (1756). He writes that 'terror is in all cases ... the ruling principle of the sublime'.

 **CHECK THE POEM**

In his 'Prelude' Wordsworth describes being awed by the brooding majesty of nature when, as he rowed on a lake at dusk, '... a huge peak, black and huge,/ As if with voluntary power instinct,/ Upreared its head'.

LINES WRITTEN A FEW MILES ABOVE TINTERN ABBEY continued

CONTEXT

In her journals Dorothy seems devoted to William. She describes him going off on a three-week trip with their brother John: 'My heart was so full that I could hardly speak to W when I gave him a farewell kiss. I sate a long time upon a stone at the margin of the lake, and after a flood of tears my heart was easier.'

CONTEXT

Dorothy outlived William by five years, dying in 1855 at the age of 83.

Line 112 is a hinge-point at which the poem moves from reflection on nature to an address to Dorothy. Wordsworth says that even without the instruction of nature, his spirits would perhaps remain 'genial' (114), because Dorothy is with him. However, while this is partly because she is his 'dearest Friend,/ My dear, dear Friend' (116–17), it is also because her 'wild ecstasies' (139) at the natural splendours of the Wye Valley echo his own feelings of earlier years. He hopes for her that these feelings will mature as his own have done, into a 'sober pleasure' (140) and that her mind will thus become 'a mansion for all lovely forms' (141). The **metaphor** here reflects the solidity and stateliness of his mature vision, in contrast to the earlier fugitive self bounding over the mountains like a man possessed. He hopes moreover that in future years, especially if she outlives him, she will remember their time together in the Wye Valley, and that the landscape was more dear to him on his second visit, for its own sake, and because he enjoyed it with her.

GLOSSARY

4	**sweet inland murmur** the River Wye is tidal well beyond Tintern, so this line proves that Wordsworth is placing himself a few miles upstream from there.
57	**sylvan Wye** bounded by woods
68	**roe** a species of deer native to Britain
77	**sounding cataract** noisy waterfall

PART THREE

CRITICAL APPROACHES

THEMES

SOCIETY AND THE INDIVIDUAL

Although Wordsworth is commonly thought of as a nature poet, he claimed that his principal concern was man, and that this was the proper concern of the poet. Coleridge is very much a social idealist, even though nature features in his poems. Thus, many of the poems in *Lyrical Ballads* explore the individual's relationship with society, and even those ostensibly about nature usually compare it with the works of man.

Some of the poems in the collection focus on characters who are cut off from society, whether by being ostracised, as in *The Rime of the Ancyent Marinere* and 'The Thorn', or through misguided choice, as in 'Lines left upon a Seat in a Yew-tree'. In extreme cases they are expelled from society altogether, as in those incarcerated in 'The Convict', 'The Dungeon' and 'The Foster-Mother's Tale'. The **narrator** of 'The Complaint of a Forsaken Indian Woman' is a special case, in that she has been abandoned by her tribe because she is too ill to keep up with them on their migration. She may be compared with another group of characters who are also, in a sense, abandoned – by a society that has the means to care for them but fails to do so. These include the main characters of 'The Female Vagrant', 'Simon Lee, the Old Huntsman' and 'The Mad Mother'. Goody Blake in 'Goody Blake and Harry Gill' also fits into this category, although she does at least get the better of her oppressor.

The Rime of the Ancyent Marinere is a wide-ranging poem with a number of important themes, but at its heart lies the Ancient Mariner's isolation from the community of his shipmates. The poem begins with him stopping a wedding guest because a wedding, with all its family associations and its role in the continuation of society, is a primary symbol of community and social cohesion. The Ancient Mariner commits a crime which results in his being ostracised, but on one level his punishment could be seen to outweigh the crime.

CONTEXT

In 1795, at the age of twenty-three, Coleridge was one of the leaders of a scheme called Pantisocracy, meaning 'The equal government of all'. Its members – twelve young men and twelve young women – planned to form a utopian community on the banks of the Susquehanna River in America.

CONTEXT

Social isolation has continued to be a major theme in literature. *The Outsider* (*L'Étranger*, 1942) by French Algerian-born novelist and philosopher Albert Camus (1913–60) is an existential novel about an alienated anti-hero who commits a senseless murder.

SOCIETY AND THE INDIVIDUAL continued

CHECK THE FILM

Cast Away (dir. Robert Zemeckis, 2000), stars Tom Hanks as a courier company technician whose plane crashes, leaving him the sole inhabitant of a desert island. Like the Ancient Mariner, he grapples with the emotional pressure of complete solitude with no prospect of rescue.

His fellow mariners, after all, are complicit in this crime: they applaud him before deciding instead to scapegoat him. At another level, however, killing the albatross is a crime against nature. The huge bird hung around his neck **symbolises** his role as the representative of Fallen Man: the albatross stands for the burden of his guilt, and of simply being human. The mariners' silent dying curse makes the anguish of his isolation all the more unbearable:

> Alone, alone, all all alone,
> Alone on the wide wide sea!
> And Christ would take no pity on
> My soul in agony. (224–7)

His shipmates' curse, it seems, is at least partly responsible for his being unable even to join them in death:

> Seven days, seven nights, I saw that curse,
> And yet I could not die. (253–4)

When finally the Ancient Mariner achieves at least a partial redemption, it is by joining the Pilot, his boy and the Hermit in their boat and then telling the Hermit his story. Yet he has to retell it from time to time, as if to renew his membership of the human community by communicating his suffering. The lesson he has learned is that it is sweet 'To walk together to the kirk/ With a goodly company!' (634–5).

CONTEXT

Strangely, Wordsworth seems to have taken the name Martha Ray from the mother of his friend Basil Montagu. She was a singer and the mistress of the Earl of Sandwich, and was shot dead outside Covent Garden Theatre by a former lover, a vicar from Norfolk.

Martha Ray in 'The Thorn' is another outcast, though in her case we are never sure whether she has committed any crime. Her scarlet cloak, particularly odd for an older woman, symbolises that she is 'fallen' – at least in the eyes of local people. For a superstitious rural community, even the fact that she was jilted by her lover and now lives alone, in poverty, is enough to make her shunned. Like the thorn tree with which she is closely associated, she is 'A wretched thing forlorn' (9). Wordsworth's gossipy **narrator** wavers between sympathy for her and identification with those who believe her to be a murderer. Wordsworth keeps us guessing as to her guilt or innocence, though her frequenting of the mound said to be her child's grave, and her reiterated cry 'Oh misery! Oh misery!/ Oh woe is me!

oh misery!' (76–7), inspire our suspicions as much as our compassion. Even when the narrator sees her and reports, 'Her face it was enough for me' (200), we cannot tell if he means that her look of grief was unbearable, or that he was afraid, or indeed if her face convinced him that the rumours were true. His repetition of local gossip and his protestations of impartiality draw us into the same climate of rumour and suspicion that condemns Martha Ray to a life of lonely isolation.

The subject of 'Lines left upon a Seat in a Yew-tree', on the other hand, can lay only a slight claim to having been rejected. In truth, society has ignored him and this has proved too much for him to bear. Rather than play a humbler role in life than he feels he deserves, he retreats into a maudlin self-pity and melancholy symbolised by the lonely yew-tree. Wordsworth makes clear the fact that he has only himself to blame:

> The man whose eye
> Is ever on himself doth look on one,
> The least of Nature's works . . . (54–6)

A more explicit contrast between natural harmony and man-made disharmony is found in 'The Convict', which begins with the poet-narrator reluctantly dragging himself away from listening to birdsong at sunset, to visit a prisoner. In the late 1790s, convicts, gaols and crime were common subjects for poetry in popular magazines, and 'The Convict' is most obviously a plea for penal reform in the popular vein. However, it is also a **gothic romance** and an **allegory** of mortality. Its **imagery** of confinement, darkness and the body point to this, as in 'The thick-ribbed walls that o'ershadow the gate' (9), which contains all three. In addition it relates to Wordsworth's view of childhood, and how its innocent joy is stifled by the advance of adulthood. The poem suffers from an excess of slightly clichéd emotive language, as in stanza 4:

> His black matted head on his shoulder is bent,
> And deep is the sigh of his breath,
> And with stedfast dejection his eyes are intent
> On the fetters that link him to death.

SOCIETY AND THE INDIVIDUAL continued

CHECK THE POEM

The convicts in 'The Convict' and 'The Dungeon' resemble Milton's fallen angels in *Paradise Lost*. In Book II, Beelzebub says of Hell, 'the King of Heaven hath doomed/ This place our dungeon, not our safe retreat'. The noble dejection of Wordsworth's convict resembles that of Milton's Lucifer.

CHECK THE POEM

Another **Romantic gothic** poem featuring a prisoner chained in a dungeon is 'The Prisoner of Chillon', by Lord Byron (1788–1824). The prisoner describes his solitude: 'I only stirr'd in this black spot,/ I only lived, I only drew/ The accursed breath of dungeon-dew.'

In addition, when Wordsworth as **narrator** introduces himself as the convict's well-wisher, the effect is to make him seem slightly naïve, or at least self-righteous. Coleridge's poem in favour of penal reform, 'The Dungeon', avoids this, and is perhaps more effective for being less concrete in its **imagery**, as well as for its use of dignified **blank verse**. It is also more concise in its depiction of the convict's suffering: 'savage faces, at the clanking hour' (14), for example. Finally, it offers a more developed recommendation for penal reform, in the form of exposure to nature. Coleridge's other poem in the collection featuring imprisonment is 'The Foster-Mother's Tale'. In this, a wrongly imprisoned youth, who has never accepted social conventions, finally escapes and disappears into a far-off land, perhaps South America, rejecting the society that has evidently rejected him.

'The Complaint of a Forsaken Indian Woman', as mentioned earlier, is a special case in the discussion of this theme. The narrator has been abandoned because if the tribe remains with her they risk their own lives. Wordsworth does not explain this, probably because he is more interested in exploring the thoughts and feelings of a woman in an appalling situation: she has lost her child and now faces a lonely death.

A final category of poems dealing with the individual and society presents characters who are in no clear way to blame for their plight. Foremost of these is 'The Female Vagrant', the most bitterly critical of the social system. Wordsworth said its aim was 'partly to expose the vices of the penal law and the calamities of war as they affect individuals' (letter to Francis Wrangham, 1795). He attacks two particular causes of agrarian decline: work moving to the cities, and the influx of new landowners with no interest in the welfare of the rural poor. Her gender is emphasised in the title of the poem, and it makes it all the more difficult for her to escape her misfortunes – which, in addition, are brought on by men: the dispossession of her father by the new landowner, and the war with the American Colonies. In her despairing sea journey and her inability to pray she resembles the Ancient Mariner, while in her grief-stricken near-madness in which she is 'robb'd of my perfect mind' (172) (the word 'robb'd' emphasising her exploitation), she brings to mind Martha Ray in 'The Thorn' and the even more disturbed narrator of 'The Mad Mother'. 'The Female Vagrant' is a vehemently anti-war poem, in its **personifications** of its horrors (**stanza** 18), and especially in the language describing its reluctant followers: '... dog-like, wading at the heels of war' (124). Moreover, despite the vagrant being a war-widow, she receives no assistance from the government. **Ironically**, she is cared for, temporarily, by other outcasts – the gypsies – although she is ultimately too morally fastidious to remain with them. The image of the poem which best sums up its condemnation of an uncaring society is perhaps the following:

> And homeless near a thousand homes I stood,
> And near a thousand tables pined, and wanted food.
> (179–80)

The other poem in the collection which especially expresses Wordsworth's sense of social indignation is 'Simon Lee, the Old Huntsman'. This old man is half-crippled by having devoted much of his active life to working as a running huntsman, facilitating the leisure pursuits of the aristocracy. Wordsworth's compassion for him is expressed in a simple description of physical details:

> And he is lean and he is sick,
> His little body's half awry
> His ancles they are swoln and thick;
> His legs are thin and dry. (33–6)

This contrasts with the emotional **rhetoric** of 'The Convict'. Wordsworth's emotional appeal is here contained more subtly, in his quiet outrage at how pathetically grateful Simon Lee is for being given a little help by a stranger, which underlies how little help he has been given by society.

QUESTION

To what extent do you regard 'The Female Vagrant' as a protest poem aiming to bring about social change, rather than one whose aim is largely to sympathise with inevitable human suffering?

CONTEXT

The ballad 'John Peel', by William Woodcock Graves, gives a favourable view of fox-hunting. It begins: 'D'ye ken John Peel with his coat so gay,/ D'ye ken John Peel at the break of day,/ D'ye ken John Peel when he's far away,/ With his hounds and his horn in the morning.' John Peel (1776–1854) was a huntsman employed by a landowner in Cumbria.

CHILD AND PARENT

To Wordsworth, childhood was virtually holy. His own childhood was a happy one, although he lost his mother when he was eight and his father five years later. The loss of his mother, especially, may well have influenced his attitude towards nature as a substitute mother, and his exploration of motherhood in his poems. Even as a young man he regarded children as being possessed not only of an innocent joy but of a kind of wisdom. In 1802 he expressed this view in 'My Heart Leaps Up':

? QUESTION

Gerard Manley
Hopkins (1844–89)
disagreed with
Wordsworth's view
of childhood, and
wrote 'The child is
father to the man.'/
How can he be? The
words are wild'
(*Poems of Gerard
Manley Hopkins*,
OUP).

My heart leaps up when I behold
    A rainbow in the sky:
So was it when my life began;
So is it now I am a man;
So be it when I shall grow old,
    Or let me die!
The Child is father to the Man;
    I could wish my days to be
Bound each to each by natural piety.

Here he reverses the usual view that children are naïve and have to learn from parents. Only a few years later he wrote regretfully in his ode 'Intimations of Immortality from Recollections of Early Childhood', 'The things which I have seen I now can see no more,' adding 'That there hath pass'd away a glory from the earth'. Later in the poem he sets out his belief:

Not in entire forgetfulness,
    And not in utter nakedness,
But trailing clouds of glory do we come
    From God, who is our home:
Heaven lies about us in our infancy!

CONTEXT

The archetype of
the Wise Fool is
found, for
example, in
Parzifal, a German
epic poem about
the Holy Grail, by
Wolfram von
Eschenbach
(c.1170–1220).

This view is nowhere more clearly embodied than in the main character of 'The Idiot Boy', who is an example of the archetypal 'Wise Fool' of folklore. Capable of only a little speech and mostly making an unintelligible 'burring' noise, he lives in a timeless world of delight in everything around him, and is simply overwhelmed by the pure joy of being sent out on horseback:

For joy he cannot hold the bridle,
For joy his head and heels are idle,
He's idle all for very joy. (82–6)

This idleness signifies more than mere inertia: here as elsewhere,
idleness is the path to mystical experience, and to joy. In 'Lines
written at a small distance from my House', the message carried from
the poet to his sister, significantly by a child, urges: 'And bring no
book, for this one day/ We'll give to idleness' (15–16). The 'idiot boy'
Johnny needs no such urging. Both poet and mother rejoice in his
natural delight: 'Oh! happy, happy, happy John' (96). When worried
about him, however, she tellingly calls him 'A little idle sauntering
thing!' (169). His natural ability to 'be' without 'doing' has now
become a liability. Yet when she finds him it is she who 'cannot move
for joy' (383) as if she has learned a lesson from her son.

Childish delight and even wisdom are also shown by the poet's son
in 'The Nightingale, a Conversational Poem'. His celestial origins
are perhaps hinted at in the words 'He knows well/ The evening
star' (92–3) and in his silent laughter at seeing the moon. There is a
hint of some intuitive knowledge, too, in the look that the Indian
woman's baby son gives her as he is taken away from her in 'The
Complaint of a Forsaken Indian Woman':

> When from my arms my babe they took,
> On me how strangely did he look!
> Through his whole body something ran,
> A most strange something did I see. (33–6)

Motherly love is, of course, closely related to the innocence and
wisdom of the child. To the unfortunate Indian woman, the loss of
her baby is far worse than the loss of her own life. Poignantly she
laments at the end of the poem:

> My poor forsaken child! if I
> For once could have thee close to me,
> With happy heart I then would die,
> And my last thoughts would happy be.
> I feel my body die away,
> I shall not see another day. (75–80)

CONTEXT

The 'evening star',
which Coleridge
says his son knows,
is Venus, seen
always at dawn or
in the evening.
Venus is associated
with beauty in all
its forms.

QUESTION

In a later version of
'The Complaint of a
Forsaken Indian
Woman' the loss of
the woman's son is
given even more
emphasis: 'But thou,
dear Babe, art far
away, / Nor shall I
see another day.'
Which version do
you prefer?

CHILD AND PARENT continued

CONTEXT

If the **narrator** of 'The Mad Mother' had entered a workhouse, she would probably have been separated from her son when he was deemed old enough, around the age of five.

CHECK THE BOOK

In 'The Mad Mother', the narrator's claim to know 'the earth-nuts fit for food' (96) is reminiscent of Caliban in Shakespeare's *The Tempest*, who initially gives Prospero and Miranda the benefit of his knowledge of the island on which they are shipwrecked. Her apparently carefree plan to live in the woods also seems to echo the woodland idyll of Sir Roland de Boys in *As You Like It*.

We have seen how devoted Betty Foy is to her 'idiot boy', even if her motherly pride in him makes her completely misjudge his ability to deliver a message. Her non-judgemental love is essential to the preservation of his joyful innocence. Less emphasis is placed on the mothering of the main character in 'The Female Vagrant'. In fact it is barely mentioned, perhaps because the thought of her dead children is unbearable. She is left '... every tear/ Dried up, despairing, desolate' (133–4). The despair which drives her temporarily mad is surely because she has lost not only her husband but all of her 'Three lovely infants' (84).

We also see less reliable mothers in *Lyrical Ballads*. The narrator of 'The Mad Mother', for example, may not be bad, but she is certainly mad, and possibly dangerous. Her devotion to her baby son is heartfelt: he is 'Sweet babe!' (11) and 'lovely baby' (15). The problem lies in her mental instability and the fact that she is dependent on the baby. Her repeated assurances, as in 'I pray thee have no fear of me' (16) and 'To thee I know too much I owe;/ I cannot work thee any woe' (19–20), raise alarm bells. No normal mother would even consider that her baby might have cause to fear her, or need to explain why she could not harm it. She claims that the birth of her baby removed her madness: 'A fire was once within my brain;/ ... But then there came a sight of joy' (21–5). This is similar to the claim made by Old Farmer Simpson in 'The Thorn' that Martha Ray, driven mad by being jilted, was restored by the baby in her womb:

> That in her womb the infant wrought
> About its mother's heart, and brought
> Her senses back again. (150–2)

In the case of 'The Mad Mother', the narrator has an abnormal need for her child:

> Suck, little babe, oh suck again!
> It cools my blood; it cools my brain. (31–2)

And later:

> Oh! love me, love me, little boy!
> Thou art thy mother's only joy. (41–2)

This is of course linked to the absence of the baby's father. The mother has been abandoned first by him, then by society. Solely responsible for the child, she risks his life and hers by carrying him 'o'er the sea-rock's edge' (44) convinced that she is somehow protected by him. More ominous still, her sudden fear of him borders on hallucination:

> – Where art thou gone my own dear child?
> What wicked looks are those I see? (86–7)

Even if she does not harm her baby in a moment of mad confusion, her intention to take him off and live in the woods is unrealistic, if not desperate.

Whereas the narrator of 'The Mad Mother' may well harm her baby, in 'The Thorn', the focus is on the rumours that Martha Ray may actually have murdered her baby. Much is made of the mound that perhaps has been heaped over its dead body, but the accusation is pure conjecture. All that can be verified, within the world of the poem, is that the woman spends long hours by the thorn tree lost in abject misery. The implication is that this is the misery of a grieving mother, but if so, whether the baby was stillborn, or died naturally in infancy, or was murdered, remains a mystery.

While Wordsworth explores motherhood in some depth, fathers are largely absent in these poems. In 'The Thorn', the possible father Stephen Hill has abandoned Martha Ray. In 'The Foster-Mother's Tale', Lord Velez is a surrogate father to the youth, but has him thrown in a dungeon. In 'The Last of the Flock' the shepherd has children but is more concerned about his sheep, even though he does sell them one by one to feed his family. In 'The Idiot Boy' the father is a woodsman who spends days at a time off in the woods at work. Where present in these poems, fathers tend to represent the rational, and Betty Foy's irrational expectations of her son are what make his adventure a **narrative** possibility. In a poem included in later editions of *Lyrical Ballads*, 'Lucy Gray', it is Lucy's rather brusque father, **symbolised** by the hook with which he cuts firewood, who sends her off to fetch her mother. He is either too careless or too unimaginative to anticipate her death in a snow storm.

CHECK THE BOOK

In *The Alphabet versus the Goddess* (Penguin, 1999) Leonard Shlain explores differences between the male and female mind, the left–right division of the brain, and how this relates to literacy. He emphasises the unconditional nature of maternal love – as shown by Betty Foy in 'The Idiot Boy'.

CHECK THE POEM

Wordsworth and Coleridge wrote other poems about children, for example Coleridge's poem about his sleeping son, 'Frost at midnight', and Wordsworth's 'Lucy' poems, such as 'She dwelt among th'untrodden ways …' (in later editions of *Lyrical Ballads*).

QUESTION

Do you feel that Wordsworth is claiming that the view of the girl in 'We Are Seven' is closer to the truth than that of her questioner?

In 'Anecdote for Fathers' the father is not neglectful, but insensitively insists on making his son justify his preferences rationally – demanding of him an adult rationalism that only makes the boy lie. In 'We Are Seven' the equally insensitive and rationalistic **narrator** repeatedly questions the girl about her dead siblings. He attempts to demean her by the repeated use of the word 'little' to describe her, but she sticks solidly to her understanding: to her, her dead siblings are ever-present. In her pre-adult innocence, she displays a kind of wisdom which contrasts with the blinkered attitude of the narrator.

On the whole, in *Lyrical Ballads*, children are portrayed as having a kind of wisdom in their innocence, mothers are mostly lovingly devoted, and fathers are either absent or not attuned to the child's outlook.

NATURE

In the poetry of the Augustans (see **Language and style: Diction**), nature is idealised as pastoral – the assumption being that city life is corrupt and rustic life innocent and carefree. There are touches of this in *Lyrical Ballads*, for example in the upbringing of the narrator of 'The Female Vagrant', and in the description of the Wye Valley in 'Lines written a few miles above Tintern Abbey'. On the whole, though, nature is not idealised in this way. It is seen as a balm and an inspiration, although one rarely finds a simple delight in the natural world without the poet drawing an overt moral lesson from it or comparing it with the works of man. Surprisingly, though Wordsworth is thought of as the nature poet of the pair, Coleridge is the author of the poem which most enthusiastically focuses on the observable details of nature, rather than nature in the abstract: 'The Nightingale, a Conversational Poem'. He captures the song of the nightingale with a sensual attention to detail that Wordsworth rarely shows:

CHECK THE POEM

Shelley's 'To a Skylark' has some realistic detail but largely focuses on the bird as a symbol of joy and inspiration: 'Like a poet hidden/ In the light of thought/ Singing hymns unbidden,/ Till the world is wrought/ To sympathy with hopes and fears it heeded not.'

> 'Tis the merry Nightingale
> That crowds, and hurries, and precipitates
> With fast thick warble his delicious notes … (43–5)

In Wordsworth's celebration of nature 'Lines written at a small distance from my House', everything speaks of joy:

Each minute sweeter than before (2)

There is a blessing in the air,
Which seems a sense of joy to yield (5–6)

Even so, there is little descriptive detail – only 'The red-breast sings from the tall larch/ That stands beside our door' (3–4). Elsewhere, Wordsworth is more concerned to express nature's beneficial effects on humanity:

Love, now an universal birth,
From heart to heart is stealing,
From earth to man, from man to earth,
– It is the hour of feeling. (21–4)

As in 'Expostulation and Reply' and 'The Tables Turned', the benefits of nature are valued above those of learning and the rational mind:

One moment now may give us more
Than fifty years of reason. (25–6)

These benefits are described more fully in other poems in the collection. In 'The Convict' Wordsworth compares the harmony of nature with the man-made horrors of the prison cell, and expresses his wish to 'plant' the convict where he will thrive (52). In 'The Dungeon', Coleridge is even more explicit in his reformist agenda, comparing the 'ministrations' of the gaolers with those of nature, whose 'soft influences' (22) and 'melodies of woods, and winds, and waters' would render the miscreant incapable of remaining 'a jarring and a dissonant thing' (24–6). He will be 'healed and harmonized/ By the benignant touch of love and beauty' (29–30). In 'Lines written a few miles above Tintern Abbey' Wordsworth explores the profound effects of nature on himself. His time spent 'in lonely rooms, and mid the din/ Of towns and cities' (26–7) hardly compares with the horrors of the convict's cell, but nonetheless he deeply values the memories of nature (specifically the Wye Valley)

CONTEXT

Wordsworth's expressed wish to 'plant' the convict at the end of 'The Convict' may mean 'plant' in the sense of having him transported to Australia, where he might start a new life. Transportation was initially introduced as a 'humane' alternative to hanging for relatively minor crimes.

CONTEXT

Wordsworth sees Dorothy as still being wildly excited by nature. In her journal, she writes of the walk that led Wordsworth to write his famous 'Daffodils': 'I never saw daffodils so beautiful. They grew among the mossy stones about and above them; some rested their heads upon these stones, as on a pillow, for weariness; and the rest tossed and reeled and danced, and seemed as if they verily laughed with the wind, that blew upon them over the lake.'

CHECK THE POEM

Another poem which passionately regrets 'what man has made of man' is William Blake's 'London' (1794), in which he writes of the 'mind-forged manacles' of civilisation.

that have provided him 'With tranquil restoration' (31). Similarly, just as Coleridge believes that nature would rehabilitate the criminal, Wordsworth feels that nature has made him a better person, performing more acts 'Of kindness and of love' (36).

In 'Lines written a few miles above Tintern Abbey' Wordsworth also makes an important point about the development of his response to nature. Once, he says, he roamed through nature with an unthinking passion and enthusiasm, experiencing 'aching joys' and 'dizzy raptures' (85–6); now he has learned to value the mystical sense of union with the infinite that nature induces in him, and to relate nature to mankind:

> For I have learned
> To look on nature, not as in the hour
> Of thoughtless youth; but hearing oftentimes
> The still, sad music of humanity.   (88–91)

Indeed, in the final words of 'Lines written in Early Spring' Wordsworth is moved by tranquil contemplation of nature's harmony to regret the disharmony of mankind:

> Have I not reason to lament
> What man has made of man? (23–4)

The paired 'Expostulation and Reply' and 'The Tables Turned' are more light-hearted but still convey a message about the benefits of nature. In the former, a rationalist intellectual friend urges the poet to stop wasting time on 'that old grey stone' (1), and read a book. Wordsworth replies that '… we can feed this mind of ours,/ In a wise passiveness' (23–4), echoing the point made in other poems that 'idleness' can profit the mind. In **stanza 6** of 'The Tables Turned' Wordsworth is explicit about the educative power of nature:

> One impulse from a vernal wood
> May teach you more of man,
> Of moral evil and of good,
> Than all the sages can. (21–4)

In some **Romantic** poetry, such as Shelley's 'Alastor, or, The Spirit of Solitude' (1816), there is an element of the sublime in the sense of that which is awe-inspiring (see **Extended commentaries: Tintern Abbey**). This appears in Wordsworth's *Prelude*, when Wordsworth describes being awe-struck – almost frightened – by a mountain at dusk, but in *Lyrical Ballads* nature is rarely anything less than benign. In 'The Mad Mother' the **narrator's** instability may lead her to fall off a cliff with her baby, and she mentions 'the poisons of the shade' (95) found in the wood – in the same breath as her baby's father. Nor does frequent exposure to nature seem to do much good for Martha Ray in 'The Thorn' or Goody Blake in 'Goody Blake and Harry Gill'. In 'Lines left upon a Seat in a Yew-tree' the situation is more complex. The proud subject appreciates nature but is somehow seduced by its beauty, so that it feeds his self-inflicted isolation rather than reuniting him with human society.

CONTEXT

The classical authors recommended by Wordsworth's intellectual friend in 'Expostulation and Reply' were the bedrock of any middle- or upper-class education in Wordsworth's day.

THE SUPERNATURAL

The theme of the supernatural appears only in a handful of poems in the collection, but it is a major theme of *The Rime of the Ancyent Marinere*. Whereas many of the poems in the collection strongly feature nature, it is questionable whether *The Rime of the Ancyent Marinere* is primarily a poem about nature or about the supernatural. In a sense it is both, because Coleridge perceives the supernatural in nature. The Ancient Mariner commits a crime against nature by killing the albatross but is punished by a spirit of the deep, who can be regarded as an elemental nature spirit or as a supernatural being. Certainly the angels that animate the mariners' corpses are supernatural, but the water snakes are living creatures, first described negatively as 'a thousand thousand slimy things' (230), then addressed as 'O happy living things!' (274). The Ancient Mariner's appreciation of their beauty is a key turning point:

QUESTION

Do you think the distinction between nature and the supernatural in *The Rime of the Ancyent Marinere* is artificial? Is 'the supernatural' the name we give to natural phenomena that we do not understand?

Within the shadow of the ship
I watch'd their rich attire:
Blue, glossy green, and velvet black,
They coil'd and swam; and every track
Was a flash of golden fire. (269–73)

THE SUPERNATURAL continued

CHECK THE FILM

The *Pirates of the Caribbean* films may owe something to *The Rime of the Ancyent Marinere* in their use of ghost ships and zombie-like sailors.

CHECK THE BOOK

A **Romantic gothic** novel with a strong supernatural theme is Mary Shelley's *Frankenstein* (1818) in which a scientist unwittingly creates a creature which comes to hate him when it feels rejected and unloved.

This moves him to bless them, and immediately he finds he can pray: so an acknowledgement of the beauty of nature results in a supernatural bounty. Elsewhere Coleridge's presentation of the supernatural is mythical: the ghastly figures of Death and Life-in-Death on the ghostly hulk.

Coleridge's theology in *The Rime of the Ancyent Marinere* is confusing, or at least ambiguous. Many aspects of the poem are Christian: the importance of the Ancient Mariner's cross being replaced by the dead albatross (shot with a *cross*-bow); his thwarted efforts to pray; his lament that 'Christ would take no pity on/ My soul in agony' (226–7); the resurrection of the mariners; and the Ancient Mariner's desire to confess to the Hermit. On the other hand there are pagan elements: the connection between the bird and the spirit of the deep; the spirit's ability to propel the boat without wind; the power of the woman representing Life-in-Death to control the Ancient Mariner; and even the druidic aspects of the Hermit. The zombie-like animation of the mariners' corpses is terrifying, tapping into deep and ancestral fears of the dead.

Elsewhere in *Lyrical Ballads* the supernatural plays a lesser role. In 'Goody Blake and Harry Gill', Harry Gill's affliction may result from a curse, or from his own fears. In 'The Foster-Mother's Tale', Lord Velez's sudden about-face, causing him to recant and cast the youth into a dungeon-like hole, is in response to what he thinks is a supernatural sign. The sudden shaking of the earth which prevents the locals from digging up the mysterious mound in the penultimate **stanza** of 'The Thorn' is very similar. In both cases, an apparently supernatural event precludes the pursuit of truth by frightening its witnesses. Lord Velez gives up questioning Christian belief, and Martha Ray's neighbours give up their plan to test her guilt.

DEATH AND LOSS

Wordsworth and Coleridge were perhaps more aware of the inevitability of death than we are in the modern age. Mortality rates were high, especially among children, and medicine was in its infancy. In addition Christian belief in heaven was not as secure as it had been. Moreover, the Romantics, as champions of individualism, were especially inclined to mourn the loss of the individual in death.

There are, arguably, no poems entirely about death in *Lyrical Ballads*, but most are at least touched by death at some level. The Ancient Mariner, of course, sees all his shipmates die before his eyes, but equally sees them ascend as souls to heaven. The subject of 'The Complaint of a Forsaken Indian Woman' faces a lonely death, and it is this that makes her thoughts profound and compelling, but she is actually more distressed by the loss of her baby son, and she has no hopes whatsoever for any sort of afterlife. Martha Ray in 'The Thorn' may be grieving for her dead baby, whether or not she is its murderer. The tragic **narrator** of 'The Female Vagrant' has lost more than any other character, and is as a consequence left as desolate as the landscape in which her questioner encounters her.

'We Are Seven' is, of course, about a child's view of death and her inability to comprehend it in an adult way. She echoes the adult euphemisms about death, saying of her sister Jane that 'God released her of her pain,/ And then she went away' (51–2), but nonetheless for her the dead siblings are still in some sense living. 'Lines written near Richmond, upon the Thames, at Evening' is in part a requiem for a dead poet, but it also celebrates the beauty of the Thames, finding in its ceaseless flow a **metaphor** for the passing of time, and of the mortality which inevitably attends it.

'The Last of the Flock' is not about death, but it is certainly a poem about loss. The shepherd seems as bereft as if he had lost his family rather than his sheep. This may be a comment on the unhealthiness of his attachment to his flock – an unhealthiness which even he acknowledges. Comparisons can be made with 'Lines left upon a Seat in a Yew-tree', whose subject is unhealthily attached to his disappointed expectations. He has allowed himself to lose the solace of human company, replacing it with lonely contemplation of a lakeside view.

CHECK THE POEM

Many poems by Thomas Hardy (1840–1928) are about death and loss. See, for example, 'In Death Divided', which begins, 'I shall rot here, with those whom in their day/ You never knew.'

LANGUAGE AND STYLE

DICTION

For many early readers of *Lyrical Ballads* the most shocking thing about it was its **diction**. Its choice of words is frequently very down-to-earth, because of the poets' desire to use ordinary language such as might be used conversationally by common people – the kind of people who are frequently the subjects or **narrators** of the poems. The choice of subject matter and the corresponding diction was in reaction to the conventionally refined subject matter and artificial, self-consciously poetic diction of the Augustan poets.

In his 1802 Preface, Wordsworth gives examples of the kind of 'poetic diction' that he and Coleridge intended to avoid. One is Thomas Gray's 'Sonnet on the Death of Mr Richard West' (1742), which begins with the following lines:

> In vain to me the smiling mornings shine,
> And reddening Phoebus lifts his golden fire
> The birds in vain their amorous descant join
> Or cheerful fields resume their green attire
> These ears, alas! for other notes repine,
> A different object do these eyes require.

The diction here is 'poetic' in the sense of being contrived in the Augustan style in a number of ways. There are inversions of the normal word order, such as beginning the first line with 'In vain' rather than placing this phrase at the end, and writing 'or other notes repine' rather than 'repine for other notes'. There is also a conventionally fanciful depiction of dawn: 'smiling mornings' and the classical **allusion** to the sun god Phoebus in the second line. The third line really means 'The birds sing pointlessly' but Gray uses poetic language – especially 'amorous descant' for birdsong. Even the phrase 'in vain' implies that the birds are actually making an effort to entertain the grieving poet. Since this is patently untrue, it reveals that Gray is describing 'poetic' birds: they are simply used as conventional decoration. The **personification**

CHECK THE POEM

Thomas Gray is best known for his 'Elegy Written in a Country Churchyard', which is much less florid in style than his 'Sonnet on the Death of Mr Richard West'. It begins, 'The curfew tolls the knell of parting day,/ The lowing herd wind slowly o'er the lea,/ The ploughman homeward plods his weary way,/ And leaves the world to darkness and to me.'

depicting the fields putting their green clothes back on is also very much the kind of unnecessary figure of speech of which Wordsworth disapproved.

Alexander Pope's 'Messiah' (1712) in the style of Virgil has similar qualities. It begins with a particularly grand appeal to classical deities and **allusions** to nature which merely set a conventionally pastoral scene without attempting to evoke any realistic picture of nature:

> Ye nymphs of Solyma! begin the song:
> To heavenly themes sublimer strains belong.
> The mossy fountains and the sylvan shades,
> The dreams of Pindus and th' Aonian maids,
> Delight no more – O thou my voice inspire
> Who touched Isaiah's hallowed lips with fire!

By and large, the poems in *Lyrical Ballads* avoid this kind of artificial language. The question, then, is what do they put in its place? First, some of the poems are, broadly speaking, **ballads**, and the language of the ballad is essentially that of ordinary people. The poem in *Lyrical Ballads* which is closest in form to the traditional ballad is *The Rime of the Ancyent Marinere*, and its language is correspondingly plain, as befits the **narrative** of an old sailor. Compare Thomas Gray's rendering of dawn, above, with Coleridge's:

> The Sun came up upon the left,
>   Out of the Sea came he:
> And he shone bright, and on the right
>   Went down into the sea. (29–32)

This is almost laughably simplistic – and no doubt many early readers did laugh. It resembles the lines quoted by Wordsworth in the 1802 Preface, written by Samuel Johnson to ridicule the efforts of poets attempting to write in the language of common speech:

> I put my hat upon my head,
> And walked into the Strand,
> And there I met another man
> Whose hat was in his hand.

CONTEXT

Pope's 'Messiah' controversially reworked parts of the Old Testament book of Isaiah in the style of the pagan Roman poet Virgil's 'Pollio'.

CHECK THE POEM

Lewis Carroll's poem 'The Walrus and the Carpenter', included in *Through the Looking-Glass* (1872), **parodied** the ballad style of poems like *The Rime of the Ancyent Marinere*: 'The sun was shining on the sea,/ Shining with all his might:/ He did his very best to make/ The billows smooth and bright −/ And this was odd, because it was/ The middle of the night.'

Coleridge's version of dawn is similar to Gray's only in the slight **personification** of the sun as 'he', which in terms of elaboration falls a long way short of Gray's 'reddening Phoebus lifts his golden fire'. Coleridge's also includes repetition, which is a feature of the folk **ballad**. This feature may have originated in magical ritual; whether or not this is the case, even this simple repetition does have a psychological power which Wordsworth comments on in the Preface and which he justifies by citing its use in the King James Bible. The simple **stanza** creates a picture of one day following on from the other in uniform succession, and may suggest the rising and falling of waves, and the pitching of a ship.

In many other stanzas, Coleridge achieves dramatic effects with equally plain **diction**. For example:

> The Ice was here, the Ice was there,
> The Ice was all around:
> It crack'd and growl'd, and roar'd and howl'd –
> Like noises of a swound. (57–60)

CHECK THE BOOK

Some of the polar effects in *The Rime of the Ancyent Marinere*, such as the noises made by the ice, resemble those described in Ernest Shackleton's account of his Antarctic expedition, *South* (1919; Penguin, 1999).

Again, repetition is used to effect, emphasising the unending nature of the ice. The lack of adornment could be taken as matching the starkness of the ice itself. However, the use of four vivid verbs for the noises it makes is striking. The noises are very different, and the use of these words one after the other, together with the repeated 'and', suggests the frighteningly strange effect of the ice on the mariners. The final line is still quite plain, if we know that 'swound' means a swoon (a fainting fit), but this **simile** suggests something more interesting: if the noises are like those half-heard on losing or regaining consciousness, the world of which they are part is on one level a world of the unconscious. Coleridge uses deceptively simple language to suggest profound ideas.

Wordsworth, too, uses some very unadorned language. In most stanzas of the 'The Thorn' there is nothing to mark it out from normal conversation apart from its use of repetition and the **metre** and rhyme scheme. For example, stanza XV:

No more I know, I wish I did,
And I would tell it all to you;
For what became of this poor child
There's none that ever knew:
And if a child was born or no,
There's no one that could ever tell;
And if 'twas born alive or dead,
There's no one knows, as I have said ...

QUESTION

How far do you find that the conversational tone of 'The Thorn' helps you to relate to the **narrator** as a realistic character?

The conspiratorial, gossipy conversational tone here is characteristic of the poem, along with the repetition of 'child', which just by its frequent use implies that there really was a child, despite the **narrator's** claim that no one could ever know 'if a child was born or no'. The use of the ''twas' in the penultimate line of this stanza makes it fit the metre but is also an example of dialect. Other examples are found elsewhere in the collection, as in Wordsworth's use of 'fiddle-faddle' in 'The Idiot Boy' (15).

Many other poems in the collection have this same simplicity of language or something close to it, including 'Goody Blake and Harry Gill', 'Simon Lee, the Old Huntsman', 'The Last of the Flock' and, to a large extent, 'The Idiot Boy'. In others the diction is more sophisticated. Take, for example, a handful of words and phrases from 'The Nightingale, a Conversational Poem': 'relique' (1), 'Distinguishes' (2), 'immortality' (31), 'venerable' (32), 'precipitates' (44), 'capricious passagings' (59). None of these is artificial – although 'relique of the sunken day' is a little fanciful, but they are all Latinate, and none would be likely to feature in the everyday speech of an uneducated person. Even in a poem about a very plain, unassuming subject, Wordsworth's 'Old Man Travelling', there are one or two slightly more sophisticated phrases than one might find in 'The Thorn' or 'Simon Lee, the Old Huntsman': 'He is insensibly subdued/ To settled quiet' (7–8) and the abstract 'mild composure' (10).

CONTEXT

Latin was the language of scholars. In addition, words derived from Latin via Norman French – the language of the conquering class in medieval England – still have associations of sophistication relative to those derived from Anglo-Saxon.

Grammatically, too, there is often more sophistication. We see this especially in 'Lines written a few miles above Tintern Abbey', in which Wordsworth's profound reflections on nature and its benefits warrant more complex **syntax**. For example:

CHECK THE BOOK

The **rhetoric** with which Wordsworth builds up to 'The dreary intercourse of daily life' resembles Shakespeare in *Hamlet*, Act III, scene 1: 'For who would bear the whips and scorns of time,/ The oppressor's wrong, the proud man's contumely,/ The pangs of despised love, the law's delay,/ The insolence of office and the spurns/ That patient merit of the unworthy takes.'

CONTEXT

In making use of **narrative,** Wordsworth and Coleridge were returning to the roots of poetry. In pre-literate societies, almost all poems told stories – usually of heroic deeds.

>   For I have learned
> To look on nature, not as in the hour
> Of thoughtless youth; but hearing oftentimes
> The still, sad music of humanity,
> Nor harsh nor grating, though of ample power
> To chasten and subdue. (89–94)

Here there is a careful use of adjectives, an unassuming yet highly effective **metaphor,** and a thoughtful use of verbs in the final line. Or there is the long yet perfectly fluent sentence in lines 122–35 beginning 'And this prayer I make'. This builds with **rhetorical** power, listing the distractions to which nature renders the individual immune, each preceded by 'nor', each longer than the previous one, until we come to the climax of 'nor all/ The dreary intercourse of daily life'. This is not the language of the common man, yet nothing here is obscure or convoluted, and there is little that resembles the flowery poeticism of the Augustans.

NARRATIVE FORM

As stated earlier, it is a feature of *Lyrical Ballads* that almost every poem tells a story. There are a few exceptions. Coleridge's 'The Nightingale' is subtitled 'a Conversational Poem' in acknowledgement of its lack of **narrative** – though even this concludes with an anecdote about Coleridge's infant son. 'Lines written at a small distance from my House' is an appeal rather than a story, and the paired 'Expostulation and Reply' and 'The Tables Turned' tell very slight stories. In 'The Dungeon' the story is implicit rather than explicit, and 'Lines written a few miles above Tintern Abbey' is largely reflective, or meditational, rather than narrative. Elsewhere the stories are a major feature even if some are not very compelling in themselves. Wordsworth himself explains this in the 1802 Preface:

> I should mention one other circumstance which distinguishes these Poems from the popular Poetry of the day; it is this, that the feeling therein developed gives importance to the action and situation, and not the action and situation to the feeling. (*Lyrical Ballads*, second edition, ed. Michael Mason, Pearson, 2007)

The story of 'Simon Lee, the Old Huntsman' is a case in point. It could be roughly summed up as follows. 'There is an old running huntsman who used to be renowned for following the hunt, but who is now half-crippled by his former work. One day I saw him trying to dig up an old tree stump. I easily got it out for him and he was pathetically grateful.' Even Wordsworth, in **stanzas** 9 and 10, acknowledges that there is not much of a tale to tell here, concluding rather self-deprecatingly with, 'It is no tale; but should you think,/ Perhaps a tale you'll make it' (79–80). However, he tellingly informs us that if we think deeply, we will find 'A tale in every thing' (76). 'The Last of the Flock' is another narrative poem which will not necessarily have readers on the edge of their seats: the poet meets a tearful man carrying a sheep; the man explains that this is the last of the flock that he has had to sell to feed his family. This simple story has the tone of a **parable**, in which the emotional content and the lesson are more important than the plot.

Other narratives in the collection are more interesting. 'Goody Blake and Harry Gill' is not a complex tale, but it is remarkable for the bizarre poetic justice of its outcome. There is also a subtle use of suspense in the descriptive detail of Harry Gill lying in wait for Goody Blake on a freezing moonlit night. 'The Idiot Boy' is remarkable for the challenge that Betty Foy sets her son, and the suspense involved in waiting to see what has become of him. The story itself is not especially complex, and Wordsworth's comments about feeling giving importance to action hold true here. We are in a sense given a non-story, because we never find out what Johnny got up to for eight hours. Instead we get a deep insight into the nature of a mother's devoted love, anxiety and relief on finding her son unharmed. In 'The Thorn', too, the story is as significant for what is not, and cannot, be told as for what is. The **narrator** toys with us, revealing the rumours of Martha Ray's supposed crime but always insisting that no one really knows the truth.

How these stories are told varies. Most are about a single main character – as in *The Rime of the Ancyent Marinere*, 'The Foster-Mother's Tale', 'The Female Vagrant', 'Simon Lee, the Old Huntsman', 'The Thorn', 'The Last of the Flock', 'The Mad Mother' and 'The Complaint of a Forsaken Indian Woman'. In

CHECK THE POEM

A later poem which, like *The Rime of the Ancyent Marinere*, has a supernatural narrative is Christina Rossetti's 'Goblin Market' (1862). Other poems with a strong narrative include Shelley's 'Alastor, or, The Spirit of Solitude' (1816), Tennyson's 'The Lady of Shalott' (1842), and Robert Browning's 'The Pied Piper of Hamelin' (1888).

NARRATIVE FORM continued

some there are two main characters, as in 'The Idiot Boy', 'Goody Blake and Harry Gill' and the adult-and-child poems 'Anecdote for Fathers' and 'We Are Seven'. Some of the tales are told in the third person, some in the first person. In the third-person **narratives** the narrator may be the poet himself, but often he takes on the voice of a **narrator**. In 'Simon Lee, the Old Huntsman', the voice seems to be very much that of Wordsworth himself telling us what may be a true story, and expressing his own sense of indignation. This also seems to be true of 'Lines left upon a Seat in a Yew-tree', though here the tone is more reflective. In 'The Thorn' he assumes the **persona** of a narrator who is definitely not himself, and who knows only part of the story he is telling, leaving the rest to our conjecture. In 'The Idiot Boy' we could easily assume that the narrator was simply Wordsworth himself, especially given the accurate biographical detail of his having been a poet 'these fourteen years' (348). However, the narrator adopts an indulgent, kindly tone, gently reprimanding Betty Foy:

> There's not a mother, no not one,
> But when she hears what you have done,
> O Betty, she'll be in a fright. (24–6)

This could almost be the voice of one of Betty's neighbours. Elsewhere Wordsworth plays with the idea of his not knowing the whole story – which adds to our sense of it being a real one. He speculates about what Johnny might be doing, complains to the Muses about their unkind refusal to give him more information (352–6), then playfully addresses the reader in the tone of a presenter on children's television: 'Who's yon, that … Sits upright on a feeding horse?' (357–61) and ''Tis Johnny! Johnny! as I live' (366).

In the first-person narratives the character of the narrator is often strongly developed. Thus we are given a powerful insight into the emotional trauma and redemptive process of the Ancient Mariner, a strong sense of the dangerous instability of the narrator in 'The Mad Mother', and of the regret and stoical suffering of the woman in 'The Complaint of a Forsaken Indian Woman'. In some poems there is an element of **framed narrative**. Thus 'The Mad Mother' begins

CONTEXT

In the 1802 Preface, Wordsworth said that he chose to write about 'low and rustic life' because 'in that condition the essential passions of the heart find a better soil in which they can attain their maturity, are less under restraint, and speak a plainer and more emphatic language'.

with a third-person description of the mother before shifting to first-person, and the narrator of 'The Female Vagrant' notionally tells her tragic tale to a near-invisible listener, present only in parenthesis in line 2, and in the final four lines of the poem. The story in 'The Foster-Mother's Tale' is told within a more formal dramatic framework, as the foster-mother's answer to a question about a mysterious entrance in the wall.

IMAGERY AND SYMBOLISM

It is a consequence of the poetic philosophy with which Wordsworth and Coleridge approached the poems in *Lyrical Ballads* that their use of **imagery** is relatively sparing, and unobtrusive. Since their aim was to write naturalistic verse that differed from good prose largely in its use of rhyme and **metre**, and which used conversational **diction**, they used imagery only insofar as the feeling generated by the content of the poem seemed to justify it. In many of the poems there was the added restriction that no image could be used that the poem's **narrator** would be unlikely to use in conversation.

Thus *The Rime of the Ancyent Marinere* contains some striking imagery, but since it is largely a first-person **narrative**, its imagery has to be plausibly in character if we are to believe in the narrator. Often this is in the form of a comparative, emphasising how extraordinary the setting is: 'And Ice mast-high came floating by/ As green as Emerauld' (51–2); 'broad as a weft' (describing the sun, 83); 'As idle as a painted Ship/ Upon a painted Ocean' (14). At all times the imagery fits the character of the Ancient Mariner himself and is evocative in a way that would have been completely foreign to Augustan sensibilities: 'We could not speak no more than if/ We had been choked with soot' (133–4).

The imagery of the plainest poems is even more sparing, and even when it occurs it is sometimes almost unnoticeable. In 'The Thorn', the tree is 'Like a rock or stone' (12); its lichen and moss make 'A melancholy crop' (15) – although there is a hint of menace in their 'manifest intent,/ To drag it to the ground' (19–20). More obvious images are very much in the folk tradition: 'the stormy winter gale/

CHECK THE POEM
Alfred Lord Tennyson makes innovative use of the **ballad** form in his early poem 'The Ballad of Oriana' (1830), and in 'The Lady of Shallot' (1842).

CHECK THE BOOK
For a study of **symbolism** in the poetry of Wordsworth and Coleridge (especially the latter), see J. Robert Barth, *The Symbolic Imagination: Coleridge and the Romantic Tradition* (Fordham University Press, 2001).

IMAGERY AND SYMBOLISM continued

CONTEXT

The scythe image in 'The Thorn' brings to mind the traditional **personification** of death as the 'Grim Reaper'.

Cuts like a scythe' (24–5), or 'It dried her body like a cinder' (131). Much the same is true of 'The Idiot Boy': the occasional **imagery** matches the homely subject matter. Johnny's lips make a sound 'As loud as any mill, or near it' (108); 'The town so long, the town so wide,/ Is silent as the skies' (255–6). More dramatically, but still naturally and appropriately: 'She darts as with a torrent's force' (384).

In the poems in which the diction is more sophisticated, there is the occasional use of a well-chosen **metaphor**. In 'Lines written a few miles above Tintern Abbey', for example, Wordsworth speaks of the 'still, sad music of humanity' (91). Later, he speaks of Dorothy's mind becoming 'a mansion for all lovely forms' (141), the image of a dignified residence fitting the maturity that he is describing.

CONTEXT

Wordsworth wrote 'The Female Vagrant' when he was twenty-one. As he became more conservative and less of an 'angry young man', he toned it down, omitting **stanza** 14, with its vivid blood-lapping imagery, altogether.

Perhaps Wordsworth's most vivid imagery occurs in his angriest poem in this collection: 'The Female Vagrant'. Here is his **narrator's** account of war:

> Better our dying bodies to obtrude,
> Than dog-like, wading at the heels of war,
> Protract a curst existence, with the brood
> That lap (their very nourishment!) their brother's blood. (123–6)

This is an extraordinary picture – human beings behaving like animals, wading in blood as they follow the war, depending on scavenging to survive. We also see in this poem several examples of **personification**, including one in the lines above, which picture war as a person, with 'heels'. Elsewhere this technique is used more obviously:

> While like a sea the storming army came,
> And Fire from Hell reared his gigantic shape,
> And Murder, by the ghastly gleam, and Rape
> Seized their joint prey, the mother and the child! (156–9)

The **simile** in the first line is plausible for the character, especially given her nightmare sea voyage to return to England. The personified 'Fire from Hell', Murder and Rape are less so, but do not seem out of place, given the extremes that the woman is describing. This is one of the few instances of personification in *Lyrical Ballads*, since Wordsworth saw this as a technique used indiscriminately by the Augustan poets in an attempt to elevate their lines to poetic stature.

Given the sparing use of imagery, and the apparently mundane nature of some of the **narratives** in these poems, **symbolism** is sometimes important, and is easy to overlook. At times its meaning is not obvious. In 'The Thorn', for example, the thorn, pond and mound assume an ominous significance through their being so frequently mentioned. The thorn can be taken as standing for Martha Ray, the pond for her emotion, and the mound for her baby – or perhaps for the rumours surrounding it. In 'The Idiot Boy', the pony relates to the boy's animal nature, while the waterfall could be seen as relating to the powerful force of a mother's love. Even in the apparently rather mundane tale of 'Simon Lee, the Old Huntsman', the old stump may be seen symbolically, perhaps as a relic of the past – the outdated feudal subservience of the poor.

Rhyme and metre

Wordsworth insists in the 1802 Preface that there does not need to be a difference in **diction** between good prose and verse. When he quotes Dr Johnson's inane stanza written to ridicule poets who wrote in prosaic language, he explains that it is the subject matter and emotional content that raise good poetry above prose. However, he does add that rhyme and **metre** play an important role in that poetry has to give pleasure, even when its content is potentially distressing – as in 'The Mad Mother' or 'The Female Vagrant' – and that rhyme and metre naturally give this pleasure. He explains that the regularity of metre 'has great efficacy in tempering and restraining the passion by an intertexture of ordinary feeling, and of feeling not strictly and necessarily connected with the passion'. In other words, metre makes distressing content bearable.

Wordsworth's explanation of why metre does this is insightful: it is to do with 'the pleasure which the mind derives from the perception of similitude and dissimilitude'. This principle can be easily seen in a

CHECK THE POEM

Shelley uses personification in a similar way to Wordsworth in his political poem 'The Masque of Anarchy', in which he personifies Murder, Fraud and Hypocrisy: 'I met Murder on the way –/ He had a mask like Castlereagh –/ Very smooth he looked, yet grim;/ Seven bloodhounds followed him …'.

CONTEXT

In the 1802 Preface Wordsworth complained of critics who on reading a line of poetry 'in which the language, though naturally arranged, and according to the strict laws of metre, does not differ from that of Prose … exult over the Poet as over a man ignorant of his own profession'.

RHYME AND METRE continued

CONTEXT

Of the two, Coleridge was probably more interested in imitating and preserving the traditional ballad form, since he adheres to it closely in *The Rime of the Ancyent Marinere* and even uses archaic words to simulate an old ballad.

simple rhyme: 'hand' and 'sand' have different beginnings and similar endings. Likewise in **metre** one finds the differences between line-lengths and stresses that make up the metre, and the broader differences between the regularity of the metre and the irregular nature of the sense of the content.

The Rime of the Ancyent Marinere follows a common ballad form: **stanzas** consisting usually of four **iambic** lines, the first and third lines with four feet, the second and fourth with three. This gives a vigorous drive, with a sense of pause after the second line and of each stanza coming to a definite conclusion. The rhyme scheme is also in **ballad** form: *abcb*. Coleridge also follows tradition in occasionally adding an extra line of four feet after the third, usually rhyming with the preceding line: *abccb*. This addition can have the effect of adding dramatic weight to the stanza, especially when Coleridge adds an internal rhyme in the fifth line:

> Under the keel nine fathom deep,
> From the land of mist and snow,
> The spirit slid: and it was He
> That made the Ship to go.
> The sails at noon left off their tune,
> And the Ship stood still also. (381–6)

This variation helps to prevent the verse from becoming monotonous, as does the occasional use of **enjambment**, as in the third line above.

None of Wordsworth's poems exactly fit the ballad metre and rhyme scheme, although many have elements of them. 'Simon Lee, the Old Huntsman', for example, consists of eight-line iambic stanzas. In some stanzas the first four lines echo the ballad metre:

> Few months of life he has in store,
> As he to you will tell,
> For still, the more he works, the more
> His poor old ancles swell. (65–8)

In others, the second line is the same length as the first, but there is still a short fourth line effectively dividing the stanza into two, as in the stanza following the one quoted above. However, Wordsworth cleverly varies the second half of each stanza by making lines 6 and 8 one syllable short. This gives a certain jauntiness to the verse. It is an indication of Wordsworth's skill that he manages to make the lines sound so natural, while sticking to the complex metre he has set himself.

'The Thorn', so stark in **diction** and **imagery**, is actually highly complex in metre. It uses an eleven-line stanza, consisting of five loosely rhyming lines and six more closely rhymed lines, rhyming *abbacc*. The rhyming **couplet** at the end of each stanza brings it to a halt, as if the **narrator** is pausing to wait for our response.

Occasionally Wordsworth's use of metre is less successful, at least to the modern reader. The bouncy **anapaestic** metre of 'The Convict' works to undermine the serious intent of the poem. Often a stronger sense of quiet dignity is found in his use of **blank verse**, as in 'Lines written a few miles above Tintern Abbey', 'Lines left upon a Seat in a Yew-tree' or 'Old Man Travelling', or where he uses the same **iambic pentameter** of blank verse but with the addition of rhyme, as in 'The Female Vagrant'. Coleridge, too, uses blank verse to stately effect in 'The Nightingale, a Conversational Poem'.

CONTEXT

Anapaestic rhythm, as used in 'The Convict', tends to sound frivolous to the modern ear, perhaps because of its use in Victorian music hall songs, and in later imitations such as 'Those Magnificent Men in their Flying Machines'.

PART FOUR

CRITICAL PERSPECTIVES

CHECK THE NET

For an excellent introduction to a wide range of critical approaches, with links, see www.kristisiegel.com/theory.htm

READING CRITICALLY

This section provides a range of critical viewpoints and perspectives on *Lyrical Ballads* and gives a broad overview of key debates, interpretations and theories proposed since the collection was published. It is important to bear in mind the variety of interpretations and responses this text has produced, many of them shaped by the critics' own backgrounds and historical contexts.

No single view of the text should be seen as dominant – it is important that you arrive at your own judgements by questioning the perspectives described, and by developing your own critical insights. Objective analysis is a skill achieved through coupling close reading with an informed understanding of the key ideas, related texts and background information relevant to the text. These elements are all crucial in enabling you to assess the interpretations of other readers, and even to view works of criticism as texts in themselves. The ability to read critically will serve you well both in your study of *Lyrical Ballads*, and in any critical writing, presentation, or further work you undertake.

EARLY RECEPTION

CONTEXT

The anonymous publication of *Lyrical Ballads* led to speculation about the identity of the authors. Similar speculation surrounded the publication of the Brontë sisters' *Poems* in 1846 under ambiguous pseudonyms.

By the end of the eighteenth century there were already at least sixty magazines that not only published poetry – including a number of poems by Wordsworth and Coleridge – but which offered reviews of new literary works to guide the choices of a growing reading public. When *Lyrical Ballads* was first published, much of the immediate commentary centred on the identity of the 'author'. Even when there was no such speculation, reviewers assumed that only one author was involved. Other reviews were divided in their assessment of the value of the poems. Some critics, as Wordsworth had predicted, hated the subject matter and style of the poems, thinking that both were unsuitable for poetry. Some liked many of the poems, admiring their simplicity and tenderness. Quite a few focused on 'The Idiot Boy', often admiring its style but deploring its subject matter. Just as many were baffled by the story of *The Rime of the Ancyent Marinere* – the inclusion of which even Wordsworth came to regret, believing that it harmed the collection as a whole. Another class of critic focused not on the style of the poems but on their politics, generally finding fault with the dangerous revolutionary social sympathies they seemed to reveal.

One of the earlier reviews was by Robert Southey, supposedly a friend of Wordsworth and Coleridge. He was, of course, aware of the identity of the authors, and wrote as follows, beginning with comments on 'The Idiot Boy':

> No tale less deserved the labour that appears to have been bestowed upon this. It resembles a Flemish picture in the worthlessness of its design and the excellence of its execution.

The other ballads of this kind are as bald in story, and are not so highly embellished in narration. With that which is entitled 'The Thorn', we were altogether displeased. The advertisement says, it is not told in the person of the author, but in that of some loquacious narrator. The author should have recollected that he who personates tiresome loquacity, becomes tiresome himself.

Southey dismissed *The Rime of the Ancyent Marinere* as lacking in unity, calling it 'a Dutch attempt at German sublimity' – perhaps thinking of the German **ballads** of Gottfried Bürger and the story of 'The Flying Dutchman'. He later wrote to a friend:

> 'The Nightingale', 'The Dungeon', 'The Foster-Mother's Tale', and the long ballad of the Old Mariner are all that were written by Coleridge. The ballad I think nonsense, 'The Nightingale' tolerable. The other two are pieces of his tragedy. For Wordsworth's poems, the last ['Lines written a few miles above Tintern Abbey'] pleases me best, and though 'The Idiot Boy' is sadly dilated, it is very well done. (To Charles Wynn, *NL* I, 176–7, 17 December 1798)

CHECK THE NET

Southey may have had in mind Flemish paintings depicting lower-class subjects such as servants. See for example Vermeer's *The Milkmaid* – go to **www. abcgallery.com** and follow the links to Vermeer.

CONTEXT

Gottfried Bürger (1747–94) was a German poet who helped to found the **Romantic** ballad tradition. He was translated into English and was a great influence on poets such as Sir Walter Scott. His most famous ballad was 'Lenore'.

Wordsworth expressed his understandable disappointment:

> ... Southey's review I have seen. He knew that I published those poems for money and money alone. He knew that money was of importance to me. If he could not conscientiously have spoken differently of the volume, he ought to have declined the task of reviewing it.

> The bulk of the poems he has described as destitute of merit. Am I recompensed for this by vague praises of my talents? I care little for the praise of any other professional critics, but as it may help me to pudding.

Southey's verdict of a considerable talent put to woeful misuse is echoed in an unsigned review in the *New Annual Register* (1798):

> The *Lyrical Ballads* ... are the productions of an author of considerable talents. ... Many of the ballads are distinguished by great simplicity and tenderness. ... With others we have been less satisfied, considering them to be unfortunate experiments, on which genius and labour have been misemployed. Of the remaining pieces some are highly beautiful and pleasing.

CONTEXT

Francis Wrangham (1769–1842) was a clergyman, poet and essayist. He also campaigned against the slave trade.

A more favourable review, attributed to Francis Wrangham, a friend of Wordsworth and Coleridge, but more likely to be by John Stoddart (1773–1856), appeared in the *British Critic* (October 1799):

> The attempt made in this little volume is one that meets our cordial approbation ... In [*Lyrical Ballads*] we do not often find expressions that we find too familiar, or deficient in dignity; on the contrary, we think that in general the author has succeeded in attaining that judicious degree of simplicity, which accommodates itself with ease even to the sublime.

The reference to 'expressions that we find too familiar, or deficient in dignity' presumably **alludes** to the reviewer's awareness that some other critics had found fault on this basis.

The reviewer for the *Monthly Mirror* (October 1798) also approved of the style of *Lyrical Ballads*:

> The contents of this little volume were 'written chiefly with a view to ascertain how far the language of conversation is adapted to the purposes of poetic pleasure'. The author has certainly accomplished his purpose, and instead of the pompous and high-sounding phraseology of the *Della Cruscan* school, has produced sentiments of feeling and sensibility, expressed without affection, and in the language of nature. If this style were more generally adopted, it would tend to correct that depraved taste, occasioned by an incessant importation from the press of sonnets and other poems, which has already made considerable inroads upon the judgment.

On the other hand, critics who found fault with the style rather than the content included an anonymous reviewer in the *Monthly Magazine* (15 January 1799):

> The author of Lyrical Ballads, has attempted to imitate the style of our old English versifiers, with unusual success; 'The Ancient Mariners', however, on which he particularly prides himself, is in our opinion, a particular exception; some of his pieces are beautiful, but others are stilted and laboured.

The reviewer for the *New London Review* (January 1799) takes issue with Wordsworth's aim of writing in a simple style, and with Wordsworth's concept of simplicity: 'The simple style has all the squalid nakedness of a beggar.' His objection is class-based:

> The language of conversation, and that too of the *lower classes*, can never be considered the language of *poetry*. What is to affect the imagination must at least address itself to the imagination; and the imagination has its peculiar style.

Finding some of the poems acceptable, this reviewer's conclusion is that the collection succeeded only insofar as it failed to achieve its own avowed aims.

CONTEXT

The Della Cruscans were a group of English and Italian poets in the late eighteenth century founded by Robert Merry (1755–98). They wrote affected, ornate poetry.

 QUESTION

Do you think there is any truth in the view that the language of *Lyrical Ballads* is too unsophisticated to inspire the imagination?

Critics who objected to the poems on social or political grounds included Francis Jeffrey of the *Edinburgh Review* (reviewing the 1802 edition of *Lyrical Ballads*), who comments on the undesirability of writing poems about members of the lower orders, and on the poets' 'perverted taste for simplicity'. The views of Dr Charles Burney (1726–1814) are similar:

> Distress from poverty and want is admirably described, in the 'true story of Goody Blake and Harry Gill'; but are we to imagine that Harry was bewitched by Goody Blake? The hardest heart must be softened into pity for the poor old woman; and yet, if all the poor are to help themselves, and supply their wants from the possessions of their neighbours, what imaginary wants and real anarchy would it not create?

QUESTION

Do you think Dr Burney has a valid point in his objection to 'The Dungeon'?

Dr Burney was even more concerned about Wordsworth's take on prison reform, as shown in 'The Dungeon':

> Here candour and tenderness for criminals seem pushed to excess. Have not jails been built on the humane Mr Howard's plan, which have almost ruined some counties, and which look more like palaces than habitations for the perpetrators of crimes? Yet, have fewer crimes been committed in consequence …?

Dr Burney was not one for subtleties of verse or hidden meaning. He was totally baffled by *The Rime of the Ancyent Marinere*, and wondered if its point was that the joke was on the wedding guest, made to miss out on the wedding banquet. As to 'We Are Seven', he regarded it as 'Innocent and pretty infantile prattle'.

James Montgomery in the *Eclectic Review* of January 1808 favourably reappraised *Lyrical Ballads* in terms of Wordsworth's aims in the Preface, speaking of the 'splendid, figurative and amplifying language' of the poems, especially 'Lines written a few miles above Tintern Abbey'.

As time went by, critical opinion of *Lyrical Ballads* was coloured by Wordsworth's increasing conservatism. There was less objection to the volume on social or political grounds, perhaps as readers saw that it was possible to sympathise with the **narrator** of 'The Female Vagrant' without actually having to campaign for social change as a result. Wordsworth's poems were coming to be seen as therapeutic rather than as dangerous or even outlandishly experimental. To some extent they were also seen as being of their time. Even the sympathetic Hazlitt hinted at this in 1825:

> It is one of the innovations of the time. It partakes of, and is carried along with, the revolutionary movements of our age; the political changes of the day were the model on which he formed and conducted his poetical experiments. His Muse (it cannot be denied, and without this we cannot explain its character at all) is a levelling one. It proceeds on a principle of equality, and strives to reduce all things to the same standard. It is distinguished by a proud humility. It relies upon its own resources, and disdains external show and relief. It takes the commonest events and objects, as a test to prove that nature is always interesting from its inherent truth and beauty, without any of the ornaments of dress or pomp of circumstances to set it off.

Appreciation of *The Rime of the Ancyent Marinere* also increased over the years. In 1818 the *Monthly Magazine* (No. 46) called it 'the finest superstitious ballad in literature', while in October 1819 Lockhart of *Blackwood's Edinburgh Magazine,* deemed it 'the wildest of all the creations of genius'. He added:

> ... the very music of its words is like the melancholy mysterious breath of something sung to the sleeping ear ... One feels that to him another world – we do not mean a supernatural, but a more exquisitely and deeply natural world – has been revealed, and that the repose of his spirit can only be in the contemplation of things that are not to pass away.

LATER CRITICISM

The belief in the music of the words of *The Rime of the Ancyent Marinere* and their almost magical power has endured for many critics, despite Wordsworth's slighting of the poem. In addition, as

CONTEXT

Hazlitt got himself into trouble when visiting Coleridge and Wordsworth in Keswick. He made improper advances to a local girl and was pursued by a mob of two hundred local men. Coleridge and Southey hid him and then sent him to safety over the mountains to Grasmere.

CONTEXT

Matthew Arnold (1822–88) was a poet, critic and cultural essayist. He wrote the poem 'The Scholar-Gipsy' and two volumes of *Essays in Criticism*.

QUESTION

How far do you feel *The Rime of the Ancyent Marinere* benefits from being seen in the context of the other poems in *Lyrical Ballads*?

QUESTION

Which do you find most prevalent in *Lyrical Ballads* – joy in nature or sadness at the human lot?

the Victorian era dawned, there was increasing approval of the poem's apparently Christian moral framework, and of the morality inherent in other poems in the collection. There was, for now, little appreciation of its importance as a key **Romantic** text. Algernon Swinburne was another Victorian critic who focused approvingly on *The Rime of the Ancyent Marinere*. In common with other critics he saw it in isolation rather than as part of *Lyrical Ballads*.

One strain of Victorian criticism saw Wordsworth as the poet of 'joy offered to us in nature, the joy offered to us in the simple, primary affections and duties' (Matthew Arnold, *Essays in Criticism, Second Series*, 1879). In the early twentieth century, A. C. Bradley offered a more sophisticated view, focusing more on Wordsworth's strangeness and paradoxes, seeing him essentially as a lone mystic, a poet of the sublimity inherent in nature, always aware of his own mortality. This divergence of views is reflected in twentieth-century appraisals, such as that of M. H. Abrams. Several critics have favoured one view of Wordsworth over the other. For example, Helen Darbishire praises Wordsworth's depiction of 'simple men and women who are moved by the great emotions' and regards *Lyrical Ballads* as 'a sort of arctic expedition, into a region where life was reduced to its elements and his aim to penetrate the heart of man and the inner life of nature' (*The Poet Wordsworth*, Clarendon Press, 1950).

New Criticism, an important movement, especially in American criticism in the period 1935–60, rejects the intentions of the author – and therefore Wordsworth's views in the Preface – emphasises the essential internal coherence of a text and attempts to resolve its paradoxes, playing down the importance of historical context. An essay in this vein by Geoffrey H. Hartman, 'Romanticism and Anti-Self-Consciousness' (1962) focuses on Wordsworth's experience of nature leading to self-knowledge, and on this as a mystical experience. In his later work, *Wordsworth's Poetry 1787–1814*, he moves away from this approach to look closely at the figures of speech and **rhetorical** forms in the poems, extracting from them the idea that Wordsworth is torn between consciousness of nature and consciousness of self, and that his poems are attempts to reconcile these.

Another development in modern approaches to *Lyrical Ballads* centres on the deconstructionist Paul de Man (1919–83), whose best-known essay on Romanticism is 'The Rhetoric of Temporality' (in *Blindness and Insight: Essays in the Rhetoric of Contemporary Criticism*, University of Minnesota, 1971). His approach, which owes much to the linguistic philosopher Jacques Derrida, sees language as essentially unstable in meaning. In this view, the language in a poem is often ambiguous, not ultimately definable, even contradictory, and dependent on internal relationships within the poem. In addition, the reader participates in creating the meaning of the text. Paul de Man objects to Geoffrey Harman's assumption that Wordsworth's key theme is the relationship between nature and the imagination.

Another strand of contemporary criticism can be traced back to Robert Mayo, who in 1954 wrote an article, 'The Contemporaneity of the *Lyrical Ballads*'. Counter to so many modern views – including that of the *Guardian* critic who compared the collection with punk rock (see **Part One: Reading Lyrical Ballads**) – Mayo argues that *Lyrical Ballads* was not particularly experimental or innovative. He points out that Wordsworth and Coleridge originally intended *The Rime of the Ancyent Marinere* to be a money-making project, and planned to publish it in the *Monthly Magazine*. It could be added that Wordsworth's objection to Southey's poor review (see **Critical perspectives: Early reception**) was that it jeopardised their chances of making money from their poems. Both Wordsworth and Coleridge were well aware of popular taste and would perhaps have been unlikely to publish a book of poems that ran completely counter to it. Mayo argues that the wide range of subjects and styles in *Lyrical Ballads* is typical of books of popular verse at that time, and that its themes of nature, simplicity and humanitarianism were commonplace in such verse:

… the more one reads the popular poetry of the last quarter of the eighteenth century, the more he is likely to feel that the really surprising feature of these poems in the *Lyrical Ballads* (as well as of many of the others) – *apart from* sheer literary excellence – is their intense fulfilment of an already stale

CONTEXT

Coleridge later criticised Wordsworth's views as put forward in the 1802 Preface, claiming that Wordsworth confused imagination with fancy. He also came to reject the view that poetic language should be that of common speech.

CONTEXT

There were a number of working-class poets active in the late eighteenth century, including John Clare, Stephen Duck (the 'Thresher Poet') and Mary Collier (the 'Washer-Woman Poet'), who wrote in local dialects.

QUESTION

How much do you think it matters whether Mayo is right about Wordsworth and Coleridge not being great innovators in *Lyrical Ballads*? Should this affect our appreciation of the poems?

convention, and not their discovery of an interest in rivers, valleys, groves, lakes and mountains, flowers and budding trees, the changing seasons, sunsets, and freshness of the morning, and the songs of birds.

For Mayo, it was not the subject matter or simple **diction** of the poems that marked them out – it was their technical mastery. The subjects of 'The Idiot Boy', 'The Female Vagrant' and even 'Old Man Travelling' would not have been outlandish to contemporary readers: they were simply members of a recognisable poetic type – the outsider. Nor is Mayo any more impressed by the poems' claim for technical innovation. Plenty of other poets had used the **ballad** form, and the versification is only original in six of the poems.

Mary Jacobus disagrees with Mayo in her *Tradition and Experiment in Wordsworth's Lyrical Ballads 1798* (1976), arguing that Wordsworth is original in his use of the language of the rustic lower classes, and in his imaginative transformation of everyday subjects and stories.

CONTEMPORARY APPROACHES

CHECK THE BOOK

Contemporary Marxist Literary Criticism by Francis Mulhern (Longman, 1992) is an anthology of criticism featuring notable Marxist critics such as Terry Eagleton and Edward Said.

A variety of other critical approaches to *Lyrical Ballads* are worth considering.

A MARXIST APPROACH

A Marxist approach to *Lyrical Ballads* would concentrate on evidence of power struggles in the poems, and on the portrayal of class oppression, as well as any hints of its resolution. Perhaps the most obvious candidate for analysis in these terms is 'Goody Blake and Harry Gill', in which the impoverished and landless Goody Blake attempts to procure for herself the basic necessities of life in the only way available to her and is as a result assaulted by the small-time landowner Harry Gill. From a Marxist viewpoint it is unfortunate that she has to appeal to God for help rather than to other members of her social class, since although she thereby gets the better of Harry Gill, her appeal in one sense reinforces her helplessness.

The angriest poem in the collection, 'The Female Vagrant', certainly lends itself to a Marxist approach. The **narrator** and her father are victims of 'new money', in the form of the landowner who has built his mansion near their home and in effect dispossesses them. Her husband's forced move to a 'distant town' (73) for work and his subsequent unemployment are all part of a process of industrialisation that benefits the capitalist employer rather than the worker. Similarly, the family's journey to America is in order that he can fight to defend the political power and commercial privilege of the British Establishment. The gypsy band which she eventually falls in with are outside of the class system, but they do not offer a realistic long-term alternative for her.

Another poem of class oppression is 'Simon Lee, the Old Huntsman'. Here, a Marxist critic might join Wordsworth in deploring the old huntsman's gratitude and lack of moral indignation after a lifetime of serving the wealthy. Even more, one could look at 'The Convict', in which the fettered prisoner both literally and **metaphorically** represents the working class, echoing the words of Jean-Jacques Rousseau (1712–78): 'Man is born free, but everywhere he is in chains' (*The Social Contract*, 1762).

A Marxist critic might also observe that, apart from Goody Blake, there are no instances of a working-class hero successfully opposing oppression in *Lyrical Ballads*. Wordsworth arouses the sympathy of his readers but does not necessarily inspire them to action.

 QUESTION

What would you expect a Marxist attitude towards the gypsies in 'The Female Vagrant' to be, given that the gypsies have opted out of conventional society, yet to some extent still depend on it?

A FEMINIST APPROACH

A Feminist approach would focus on the role of women in the poems. *The Rime of the Ancyent Marinere* depicts an entirely male world. After the passing mention of the bride, only the ship is female, until we meet the ghastly figure of the woman representing Life-in-Death playing dice with Death on the ghostly hulk. She is an extremely negative depiction of femininity, given her macabre appearance, and the fact that she takes control of the Ancient Mariner.

A FEMINIST APPROACH continued

CHECK THE BOOK

Some authors, for example Hunter Davies in his biography of Wordsworth, have suggested that Dorothy may have had a significant role in the composition, or at least the inspiration, of Wordsworth's poems.

QUESTION

Love poems are notably absent from *Lyrical Ballads*. Do you think that Wordsworth's emotional needs were largely fulfilled by Dorothy, and by nature?

'The Female Vagrant' would be as much of a focus for Feminist criticism as for a Marxist approach. As a woman, the **narrator** is very much in the shadow of men in the **narrative**. Even in the first line she describes her home as 'my Father's cottage', and her father's fortunes determine her own. She is apparently not at liberty to follow her lover when he moves to the town, and then has no choice but to follow him to war once he is her husband. Throughout, she is a victim of male-dominated society. She can only rebel in the fierce language she uses to describe war, and in eventually choosing to follow her conscience and leave her gypsy friends.

Even in poems with less of a story to tell, Feminist critics might question Wordsworth's attitude towards women. He is perhaps rather patronising in 'Lines written a few miles above Tintern Abbey' when he compares Dorothy's 'wild ecstasies' (139) with his own supposedly more mature attitude to nature.

Feminist criticism might also focus on the theme of motherhood in the poems. There are no really positive portrayals of motherhood: Wordsworth's mothers tend to be mad, criminal or deprived of their children. In the case of 'The Female Vagrant', we barely see the narrator with her children before they are snatched away by war; in 'The Complaint of a Forsaken Indian Woman' the narrator has had to give up her child. In 'The Idiot Boy' the mother is completely devoted to her son, but even Wordsworth, as narrator, questions her wisdom in sending him out at night on horseback to carry a message to the town. As to 'The Mad Mother', we may sympathise with the narrator, abandoned by the child's father, but we could also see her as a projection of negative male expectations of women.

A PSYCHOANALYTICAL APPROACH

The poems also lend themselves to some extent to interpretation based on Freudian and post-Freudian psychology. The narrator of 'The Mad Mother' could be seen as embodying infant fears of being destroyed by the all-powerful mother, as well as the mother's own ambivalence about her baby: she seems to swing from neediness to fearing his 'wicked looks' (86). Such an approach might also look at the negative portrayal of women in *The Rime of the Ancyent Marinere* (see **A Feminist approach** above), and at the whole range of **symbolism** in that poem. The poem could be seen as embodying a sense of primal guilt, symbolised by the albatross, with the elemental spirit representing a punitive father figure, and the Hermit a benign father figure.

Such an approach might also look at the split between loving and dangerous mother figures in Betty Foy and the narrator of 'The Mad Mother'. In a broader sense, one could also explore Wordsworth's attitude towards nature, which seems to be a substitute mother for him, especially in poems such as 'Lines written in Early Spring' and 'Lines written a few miles above Tintern Abbey'.

A NEW HISTORICIST APPROACH

New Historicism emerged in reaction to linguistic or formal approaches to literature which insisted on seeing a text in isolation. A New Historicist approach to *Lyrical Ballads* would have a certain amount in common with a Marxist one, seeing the collection in terms of its historical context and looking at the involvement of the poems with the power relations of their time. The American strand of this approach would see poems such as 'The Female Vagrant' as providing an outlet for political dissent rather than provoking it. *The Rime of the Ancyent Marinere* would be a particularly interesting case, as it is of its time yet looks back to an earlier age. In its depiction of a hero essentially lost at sea, and in its harking back to an earlier time, it could be seen as reflecting the social upheavals brought about by the French Revolution.

CONTEXT

The psychoanalyst Donald Winnicott (1896–1971) saw one role of the mother in a healthy child's development as being to provide a 'holding environment' for the child in which it is protected without knowing it, and to allow the child to express negativity towards the mother without her rejecting the child.

PART FIVE

BACKGROUND

WILLIAM WORDSWORTH

William Wordsworth was born at Cockermouth, Cumbria, the son of a lawyer. He went to the infants school in Penrith, where another of the pupils was Mary Hutchinson, whom he was later to marry. His mother died in 1778 when he was only eight years old – a factor which may have influenced his poetry. From 1779 he attended Hawkshead Grammar School with his brother John, boarding with an elderly couple, the Tysons. Mrs Tyson became a mother figure to the two boys, and to the two younger brothers who followed later. Luckily for William, he was allowed a lot of freedom, and spent much of his free time wandering over the fells.

Five years after the death of his mother, the young Wordsworth had another loss to bear: his father John lost his way in bad weather while riding home and was forced to spend a night without shelter on Cold Fell. He caught a severe chill from which he never recovered. Unfortunately for the family it was discovered that John Wordsworth had not claimed his salary from his employer, Sir James Lowther, for several years – and it soon became apparent that Lowther had no intention of paying it to his heirs. This blighted William's early life, leaving him impoverished and dependent on friends and benefactors.

Wordsworth attended St John's College, Cambridge, but was unhappy there, developing a low opinion of the tutors, whom he described as 'grotesque in character', and hating the maths-based honours course. He was equally dismissive of the dissolute students. In 1790, while still a student, he went on a walking tour of France, the Alps and Italy, and was particularly excited by France. After achieving an undistinguished degree in 1791, he returned to France, spending a year there. He became an enthusiastic believer in the cause of the Revolution, which had begun two years earlier. He also fell in love with the daughter of a surgeon, Annette Vallon, who

CONTEXT

Wordsworth's first poetry was composed as a school exercise when he was fourteen. The set subject, still a favourite with teachers, was 'What I did in my summer holidays'.

CONTEXT

The poet Thomas Gray had protested about the emphasis on maths at Cambridge. It dated back to the influence of its most famous student, Isaac Newton (1643–1727).

became pregnant and bore him a daughter, Caroline, in 1792.
Contrary to the popular belief that he simply abandoned mother
and child, he evidently intended to marry Annette and kept in
correspondence with her (with his sister Dorothy's help), but was
prevented from returning to France because it became too
dangerous once France and Britain were at war. A series of touching
love letters between the young couple survive, providing evidence
of Wordsworth's good intentions. The public never knew about this
affair during his lifetime, and Wordsworth scholars were
understandably shocked and delighted when the evidence emerged
in the twentieth century.

In 1795 Wordsworth received a legacy of £900 from a friend,
Raisley Calvert. This money came at a price, however. Wordsworth
and Calvert were not especially close, but Wordsworth felt duty-
bound to stay with the dying young man in Keswick when he
would rather be elsewhere. The money did enable him to be
reunited with Dorothy, however. They lived first at Racedown in
Dorset, then in Alfoxden in Somerset, where they looked after the
son of their friend Basil Montagu. Wordsworth made the move to
Somerset in order to be near Coleridge, who lived at Nether
Stowey. After producing the great literary landmark that was *Lyrical
Ballads*, Wordsworth visited Germany, where he wrote much of
what was to become his great autobiographical poem, *The Prelude*.
He and Dorothy went to live in Dove Cottage in Grasmere in 1799.

In 1802 Wordsworth decided to get married to Mary Hutchinson.
This was partly because he felt free to do so, as the Lowther money
was finally on the verge of being paid out – Sir James had died and
his son was more kindly disposed towards creditors than his father
had been. However, always a man of honour, Wordsworth felt he
had to visit France and square this plan with Annette, and he took
advantage of the year-long Peace of Amiens to do so. Wordsworth
and Dorothy travelled to Calais and met Annette, spending four
weeks there with her. After that, Wordsworth returned and married
Mary. Thereafter he lived with wife and sister in what, surprisingly,
seems to have been domestic bliss.

> **CONTEXT**
>
> Wordsworth
> wrote: 'I begin to
> wish much to be in
> town; cataracts
> and mountains are
> good occasional
> society, but they
> will not do for
> constant
> companions,
> besides I have not
> even much of their
> conversation as I
> am so much with
> my sick friend and
> he cannot bear the
> fatigue of being
> read to.'

It was also in 1802 that Wordsworth began 'Intimations of Immortality', published in 1807 along with many other of his most famous lyric poems. He became the father of five children, and cultivated new friendships, with the novelist Sir Walter Scott, the patron of the arts Sir George Beaumont, and Thomas De Quincey. He was gradually becoming more conservative in outlook and taste, having long since abandoned his youthful revolutionary fervour. He even joined the local reserve militia, a patriotic move applauded by Beaumont. Wordsworth's popularity increased and his reputation became more firmly established, ironically more or less as his real inspiration was waning. In 1827 he was left a legacy by Beaumont, and in 1842 was awarded a Civil List pension of £300 per annum. In 1843 he was made Poet Laureate, a post which he enjoyed until his death in 1850.

SAMUEL TAYLOR COLERIDGE

Samuel Taylor Coleridge was born in 1772, the youngest son of a Devonshire vicar. After his father died, Samuel was sent to Christ's Hospital, a charitable boarding school in London, where Leigh Hunt and Charles Lamb were among the young admirers of his precocious eloquence. At Cambridge (1792–4), where he was a heavy drinker and political firebrand, a broken heart led him to enlist in the Army under a false name. His brothers bought him out, but he left university without a degree.

In 1794 Coleridge met Robert Southey and together they founded Pantisocracy, a socially idealistic group of young men and women who intended to found a utopian commune in America. To fund this venture, Coleridge published political poems in the *Morning Chronicle* and, with Southey, gave a series of lectures in Bristol. The pair also collaborated on a drama, *The Fall of Robespierre* (1794), and courted and married two sisters, Sara and Elizabeth Fricker. Sara soon became the mother of Coleridge's first son, Hartley. At this time Coleridge was preaching throughout the West Country, and considered becoming a Unitarian minister. In addition, however, he was beginning to use opium in periods of illness (or hypochondria) and depression.

According to some accounts, Coleridge met Wordsworth in Bristol after one of Coleridge's lectures; according to others, they first met when Coleridge walked to Racedown, Dorset, where Wordsworth was living with Dorothy. Whichever is the case, the two men embarked on a friendship and a literary collaboration which led to the publication of *Lyrical Ballads*. In 1797–8 they lived two miles apart on the edge of the Quantock Hills in Somerset, Coleridge in Nether Stowey and Wordsworth in Alfoxden. They spent a great deal of time together walking, discussing literature, and composing poetry. It was here that they were investigated on suspicion of being spies for Revolutionary France. It was also here that Coleridge wrote his drama *Osorio*, from which 'The Foster-Mother's Tale' was later extracted for use in *Lyrical Ballads*.

Coleridge was deeply interested in German philosophy, and spent ten months in Germany in 1798–9, studying Immanuel Kant, Schiller and Schelling. He moved to the Lake District in 1800 to be near the Wordsworths, and fell in love with another Sara – Wordsworth's future sister-in-law. Meanwhile he was becoming increasingly dependent on opium, which he took in the form of laudanum. Attempting to restore his health, Coleridge travelled abroad and worked in Malta for two years. He finally separated from his wife Sara in 1807 and once again went to live with the Wordsworths, and his new love, Sara Hutchinson. His happiness was brief. Increasingly ravaged by opium, he fell out with the Wordsworths, and was abandoned by Sara, who moved to Wales. Seriously depressed, Coleridge moved to London, where he was sustained by only a few friends. He did, however, manage to deliver a series of lectures on Shakespeare during the winter of 1811–12.

In 1813–14 Coleridge experienced a rebirth of his Christian faith, and began to free himself from opium. This enabled him to write and publish an important semi-autobiographical work of philosophy and literary criticism, *Biographia Literaria*. It was his *Christabel and Other Poems* (1816), however, that established him as a literary giant, at least in the eyes of younger poets. As he grew older, he wrote less poetry of note, focusing more on philosophical and religious writings. He died of a heart attack in 1834.

CONTEXT

A Home Office investigator stood behind hedges listening to the supposedly seditious conversations of Wordsworth and Coleridge. Hearing them discussing the philosopher Spinoza, he reported that they had been talking about 'Spy Nozy'.

CONTEXT

Laudanum was prescribed by doctors as a painkiller, and for a variety of conditions, from the seventeenth to the early twentieth century. Many people took it medicinally and then became addicted. Victorian users included De Quincey, Dickens, Elizabeth Barrett Browning and Wilkie Collins.

HISTORICAL BACKGROUND

The years leading up to the publication of *Lyrical Ballads* in 1798 were momentous ones for Europe and for Britain. The American colonies had long begun to harbour anti-British, separatist sentiments, though much of the population still wanted to remain under British rule. The king, George III, strongly resisted any compromise over the colonies, and tension came to a head with the Boston Tea Party in 1773, when British-taxed tea was thrown into Boston Harbour by protesting Americans. Open war broke out in 1775, with the French supporting the American colonists, and many Native American tribes siding with the British. The war ended in 1782, with the colonies achieving independence, though Canada remained British. Britain had lost troops and revenue, and was left economically weak. Soldiers returned home penniless and jobless, to swell the ranks of a growing underclass of the discontented.

When the French Revolution broke out in 1789, it was hailed by **Romantic** poets and many British radicals as the best thing that could have happened to France, and even to Europe. To some it was the dawn of a new era, when tyrants would be overthrown, the poor would cease to be oppressed, and human beings would be able to achieve their full potential in a great brotherhood of man. Needless to say, the Tory Establishment saw things differently. The fall of the Bastille (14 July 1789) was regarded by radical sympathisers across Europe as a blow for liberty. Gradually the festive mood that Wordsworth had experienced on his first visit to France in 1791 gave way to a grimmer one. In December 1792 Louis XVI was brought to trial. He went to the guillotine in January 1793. His queen, Marie-Antoinette, suffered the same fate the following October.

Once Robespierre rose to power, the executions increased, to the growing horror of former sympathisers. The more moderate revolutionaries Danton and Desmoulins were guillotined in 1794. Robespierre himself was executed a few months later. No one was safe: the revolution had turned into a bloodbath. From 1795, republics were established in other parts of Europe, but at the same time Napoleon Bonaparte was rising to power in France. By 1799 he was effectively in charge of the country, as First Consul. Five years later he crowned himself Emperor.

Wordsworth and Coleridge watched with dismay as the republican dream turned to nightmare, hoping briefly that Napoleon would save the situation, only to see him become a new despot. Meanwhile, Britain was at war with France, and the Tory government's answer to political unrest was simply more repression. Even as the rural poor became poorer, the once radical Wordsworth became increasingly conservative, partly because of the changes that often come with age and increased affluence, but also in reaction to the bloodshed of the French Revolution. Coleridge's sympathies underwent a similar though less marked transformation.

LITERARY BACKGROUND

INFLUENCES ON WORDSWORTH AND COLERIDGE

Like other educated men of their era, Wordsworth and Coleridge were well schooled in the works of classical Roman and Greek authors. These same authors, especially Romans such as Horace, Virgil and Ovid, had been regarded as the models of poetic style by most of the notable poets of the hundred years or so before Wordsworth and Coleridge came to prominence – including Dryden, Pope, Goldsmith and Thomson. These poets, the Augustans, named after the Roman Emperor Caesar Augustus (63BCE–19CE), during whose lifetime they lived, had a particular set of views on what was appropriate in terms of the subject matter and style of poetry. In their opinion, poetry was an elevated art form, and its subjects should be similarly elevated. There is not a single character in *Lyrical Ballads* whom the Augustans would have deemed worthy of poetic effort.

> **CONTEXT**
>
> Ovid (43BCE–CE17) is probably most famous for his *Metamorphoses*, a **narrative** poem in fifteen volumes which tells the story of the creation of the world and its history.

Likewise, when it came to style, the language of poetry was that of the educated upper class. Its **diction** was formal, fanciful and full of **personification** (for examples, see **Language and style: Diction**). Wordsworth, on the other hand, argued in the Preface to the 1802

INFLUENCES ON WORDSWORTH AND COLERIDGE continued

edition of *Lyrical Ballads* that the lives of the rustic lower classes were actually better subjects for poetry than those of the wealthy, because they were unpretentious and closer to the essential nature of human emotion. Moreover, the language of the relatively poor was better suited to poetry, because it was more in tune with true emotion, and because its simplicity was more sincere than the language of the fashionable rich.

Wordsworth's Preface was the first serious attempt by a poet to explain and justify his methods; in a sense the first real document of literary analysis. In it he said that he wanted to describe ordinary incidents from common life, 'in a selection of language really used by men'. He insisted that all of the poems in *Lyrical Ballads* had a 'worthy purpose'. Poetry, he said, was the 'spontaneous overflow of powerful feelings', but that these had to be tempered by thought. In these poems, feeling would give importance to action, and not action to feeling. The poet's first duty was to give pleasure, for example by the use of rhyme and **metre**. Only by doing this could he hope to elevate the moral sense of the reader.

THE INFLUENCE OF *LYRICAL BALLADS* ON LATER POETS

In a broad sense, the focus on ordinary incidents and poor people, and the use of plain language, has been a huge influence on poetry right up to the present day. Closer to the era, Shelley and Keats were influenced by Wordsworth, especially in their taking inspiration from nature. However, neither of them makes a religion of nature in the way that Wordsworth does. When Shelley writes about nature, he sees something awe-inspiring, outside of man, almost threatening, whereas Wordsworth sees nature as being inherently in tune with the highest expression of the human soul, capable even of rehabilitating the convict. Both Shelley and Keats are perhaps more influenced by the lyricism of Coleridge than by Wordsworth's starker poems, such as 'The Last of the Flock'.

The poems of Wordsworth were a great influence on all three Brontë sisters and their brother Branwell, who wrote a sycophantic letter to Wordsworth in the hope of promoting his own poetry. The

CONTEXT

Shelley's *Defence of Poetry*, written in 1821 and published posthumously in 1840, is more theoretical than Wordsworth's 1802 Preface, focusing on the nature of imagination and the role of the poet rather than on the language of poetry. He calls poets 'the unacknowledged legislators of the world'.

poems of Emily and Anne, however, have more in common with Wordsworth's. His plain **diction** and feeling for nature as a source of moral truth can be compared with Emily's **pantheistic** poems, such as 'Loud without the wind was roaring' and 'The blue bell is the sweetest flower'. Her poem 'Alone I sat', with its reference to 'The solemn joy around me stealing/ In that divine untroubled hour' seems to echo Wordsworth's visionary poems, such as 'Lines written in Early Spring'.

Thomas Hardy was probably more influenced by Wordsworth's bleakest poems than were Shelley and Keats. Hardy's 'Drummer Hodge', for example, is about a common soldier who has died in South Africa. With its plain diction matching its subject, it has echoes of 'Simon Lee, the Old Huntsman'. Some of Hardy's heroines, lower class but virtuous women like Tess Durbeyfield, have much in common with the **narrators** of 'The Female Vagrant' and 'The Mad Mother'. Wordsworth's underprivileged male characters, too, have their echoes in the rural poor of Hardy's novels.

A number of more modern poets have been influenced by Wordsworth, whether directly or indirectly. Ted Hughes (1930–98) wrote many poems about nature, though he focused more on its raw energy than on its powers of mystical inspiration. R. S. Thomas (1913–2000) wrote about rural life, and the rural poor in a way that has some echoes of Wordsworth. Others, such as Philip Larkin (1922–85) and Simon Armitage (b. 1963) have further developed the use of a diction based on everyday speech.

CHECK THE BOOK

Thomas Hardy's *Tess of the D'Urbervilles* (1891) tells the story of a young woman seduced by a wealthy but immoral young man. She marries an apparently more virtuous man who nonetheless abandons her when she reveals her past.

CHECK THE BOOK

Simon Armitage (b. 1963) is one modern poet who writes in an ordinary conversational style using first-person **narration**. See, for example, 'Hitcher' and 'I am very bothered when I think'.

World events	Wordsworth and Coleridge's lives	Literary events
	1770 Wordsworth born	**1770** William Goldsmith, *The Deserted Village*
	1771 Sister Dorothy born	
	1772 Coleridge born	
1773 Boston Tea Party		
		1774 Robert Southey born
1775 Britain at war with American colonies		**1775** Charles Lamb born
	1776–7 Wordsworth attends infant school at Penrith (with Mary Hutchinson)	
	1778 Wordsworth's mother dies; he attends Hawkshead Grammar School	
1782 American Independence	**1782–91** Coleridge at Christ's Hospital School	
1783 William Pitt the Younger Prime Minister	**1783** John Wordsworth (father) dies	**1783** William Blake, *Poetical Sketches*
		1784 Death of Samuel Johnson
		1786 Robert Burns, *Poems*
	1787 Wordsworth enters St John's College, Cambridge	
1789 French Revolution		**1788** Lord Byron born
		1789 Blake, *Songs of Innocence*
	1790 Wordsworth on European walking tour	

World events	Wordsworth and Coleridge's lives	Literary events
	1791 Wordsworth leaves Cambridge with BA; Coleridge at Jesus College, Cambridge	
	1792 Wordsworth in love with Annette Vallon; daughter Caroline born	**1792** P. B. Shelley born
1793 Louis XVI, then Marie-Antoinette, executed	**1793** Wordsworth on walking tour of South-West England and Wales	
1794 Execution of Danton, Desmoulins, Robespierre	**1794** Coleridge forms Pantisocracy with Southey, gets engaged to Sara Fricker, leaves Cambridge; writes *The Fall of Robespierre* with Southey	**1794** Blake, *Songs of Experience*
	1795 Raisley Calvert dies, leaving Wordsworth £900; Wordsworth and Dorothy settle in Dorset; Wordsworth and Coleridge meet; Coleridge lecturing in Bristol and marries Sara; publishes *Poems on Various Subjects*; takes opium for first time	**1795** John Keats born
		1796 Death of Burns
	1797 Wordsworth and Coleridge engage in intense joint poetic activity; *Lyrical Ballads* planned; Wordsworth and Dorothy move to Alfoxden; Wordsworth finishes 'Margaret, or the Ruined Cottage'; Coleridge writes *Osorio* and preaches in South-West	

World events	Wordsworth and Coleridge's lives	Literary events
	1798 *Lyrical Ballads* published; Wordsworth visits Germany; Coleridge writes 'Kubla Khan'	**1798** Walter Savage Landor, *Gebir*
1799 Napoleon First Consul	**1799** Wordsworth in Germany writing *The Prelude*; he and Dorothy settle in Dove Cottage, Grasmere	
	1800 Coleridge visits Dove Cottage with family, then settles in Greta Hall; Wordsworth writes *The Recluse* (Book I), 'The Brothers', 'Michael', *Poems on Naming of Places*	**1800** Robert Burns (d. 1796), *Works*
	1801 *Lyrical Ballads* second edn published	**1801** Robert Southey, *Thabala the Destroyer*
1802 Napoleon Emperor of France	**1802** Wordsworth writing *The Excursion*; he visits Annette at Calais, with Dorothy, then marries Mary Hutchinson; *Lyrical Ballads* third edn	**1802** Walter Scott, *Minstrelsy of the Scottish Border*
	1803 Son, John, born to Wordsworths	
	1804 Wordsworth writing *Prelude*; Dora Wordsworth born; Coleridge works in Malta, visits Sicily, Rome and Naples	**1804–20** Blake's *Jerusalem*
1805 Battle of Trafalgar	**1805** *Prelude* finished; John Wordsworth (brother) drowned; *Lyrical Ballads* fourth edn	**1805** Scott, *The Lay of the Last Minstrel*; Southey, *Madoc*
	1806 Son Thomas Wordsworth born	**1806** Elizabeth Barrett Browning born; Byron, *Fugitive Pieces*

World events	Wordsworth and Coleridge's lives	Literary events
	1807 Wordsworth's *Poems in Two Volumes* (savaged in *Edinburgh Review*); Coleridge meets De Quincey, who gives him £300	**1807** Southey, *Letters from England*
	1808 Wordsworths move to Allan Bank; Coleridge and De Quincey visit	
	1809 Coleridge, *The Friend*	**1809** Edgar Allan Poe born
	1810 William Wordsworth (son) born; Coleridge and Wordsworth estranged	**1809** Alfred Tennyson born
		1811 Jane Austen, *Sense and Sensibility*
	1812 Wordsworth and Coleridge reconciled	
	1813 Wordsworth appointed stamp distributor for Westmoreland; Coleridge's play *Remorse* performed; Coleridge lectures on Shakespeare and Milton	
1814 Napoleon banished to Elba		**1814** Austen, *Mansfield Park*; Scott, *Waverley*; Wordsworth, 'The Excursion'
1815 Napoleon escapes but is beaten finally at Waterloo	**1815** First collected edition of Wordsworth's poems	**1815** Byron, 'Hebrew Melodies'
	1816 Coleridge's *Christabel and Other Poems*	**1816** Austen, *Emma*; Shelley, 'Alastor'
	1817 Wordsworth meets Keats; Coleridge, *Biographia Literaria*	**1817** Keats, *Poems*

World events	Wordsworth and Coleridge's lives	Literary events
		1818 Austen's *Northanger Abbey* and *Persuasion* published; Byron, *Don Juan*; Keats, 'Endymion'; Scott, *Heart of Midlothian* and *Rob Roy*; Mary Shelley, *Frankenstein*
1819 Birth of future Queen Victoria; 'Peterloo' Massacre, Manchester		
1820 George III dies; succeeded by Prince Regent, George IV	**1820** Wordsworth on European tour	**1820** Keats, 'Ode to a Nightingale'; Scott, *Ivanhoe*; Shelley, 'Prometheus Unbound'
1821 Cato Street Conspiracy against Cabinet		**1821** Keats dies; commemorated in Shelley's 'Adonais'
1822 Turks invade Greece; suicide of Foreign Secretary, Castlereagh	**1822** Wordsworth, *Description of the Scenery of the Lakes*	**1822** Shelley dies
		1824 Byron dies in Turko-Greek War; Scott, *Redgauntlet*
1827 Turks enter Athens		
1828 Duke of Wellington becomes Prime Minister	**1828** Wordsworth, Dora and Coleridge go on tour of Rhine; Coleridge, *Poetical Works*	**1828** Scott, *Tales of a Grandfather* and *The Fair Maid of Perth*
		1829 Tennyson, 'Timbuctoo'
1830 Revolution in Paris; in Britain William IV succeeds George IV		**1830** Emily Dickinson and Christina Rossetti born; Tennyson, *Poems, Chiefly Lyrical*

World events	Wordsworth and Coleridge's lives	Literary events
		1831 Poe, *Poems*
1832 Reform Act doubles number of voters		**1832** Scott dies; Tennyson, 'The Lady of Shalott'
		1833 Hartley Coleridge, *Poems*
	1834 Death of Coleridge	**1834** Lamb (essayist) dies
		1835 Robert Browning, 'Paracelsus'
		1836 Charles Dickens, *Pickwick Papers*
1837 William IV succeeded by Victoria		
1838 First Chartist petition presented		**1838** E. B. Browning, *The Seraphim and Other Poems*
1839 Coronation of Queen Victoria		**1839** H. W. Longfellow, 'Hyperion' and 'Voices of the Night'; Poe, *The Fall of the House of Usher*
1840 Victoria marries Prince Albert		**1840** R. Browning, 'Sordello'
1841 Lord Melbourne (Whig) succeeded as Prime Minister by Peel (Tory)		**1841** Dickens, *The Old Curiosity Shop*
1842 Riots and strikes in north of England	**1842** Wordsworth granted Civil List pension of £300 p.a.	**1842** Poe, 'The Masque of the Red Death'
	1843 Wordsworth made Poet Laureate	**1843** Southey dies; Tennyson, 'Mort d'Arthur', 'Locksley Hall'

World events	Wordsworth and Coleridge's lives	Literary events
1845 Start of Irish Famine		
		1846 Publication of *Poems*, by 'Currer, Ellis, and Acton Bell' (the Brontë sisters)
		1847 Charlotte Brontë's *Jane Eyre*; Anne Brontë's *Agnes Grey* and Emily's Brontë's *Wuthering Heights*
1848 European revolts, including Paris		**1847–8** W. M. Thackeray, *Vanity Fair*
		1848 Elizabeth Gaskell, *Mary Barton*
1849 Disraeli leader of Conservative Party	**1849** Wordsworth's *Poems in Six Volumes*	**1849** Dickens, *David Copperfield*
	1850 Wordsworth dies	**1850** E. B. Browning, *Sonnets from the Portuguese*; Tennyson made Poet Laureate
		1851 Herman Melville, *Moby Dick*
1852 Duke of Wellington dies		**1852** Dickens, *Bleak House*
1853 Crimean War begins		**1853** Matthew Arnold, 'The Scholar Gypsy'; Gaskell, *Ruth* and *Cranford*
		1854 Tennyson, 'The Charge of the Light Brigade'
	1855 Dorothy Wordsworth dies	**1855** R. Browning, *Men and Women*; Longfellow, *The Song of Hiawatha*; Tennyson, 'Maud'; Walt Whitman, *Leaves of Grass*

THE WORKS OF WORDSWORTH AND COLERIDGE

Coleridge's Notebooks: A Selection, ed. Seamus Perry, OUP, 2002

Poetical Works of Samuel Taylor Coleridge, ed. E. H. Coleridge, OUP, 1912

Poetical Works of William Wordsworth, ed. Ernest de Selincourt, OUP, 1904

Samuel Taylor Coleridge: Selected Poetry, ed. William Empson and David Pirie, Fyfield Books, 1989

Wordsworth and Coleridge: 'Lyrical Ballads', ed. R. L. Brett and A. R. Jones, second edn, Routledge, 2001

Wordsworth and Coleridge: 'Lyrical Ballads', ed. Michael Mason, second edn, Pearson, 2007
    Includes the 1802 Preface, numerous accompanying statements by both authors; well annotated throughout

LETTERS AND BIOGRAPHY

Hunter Davies, *William Wordsworth,* Atheneum, 1980
    Very readable account focusing on the life rather than the poems

Stephen Gill, *William Wordsworth: A Life,* Oxford Paperbacks, 1990
    Interrelates the life and the work

E. L. Griggs, *Letters of Samuel Taylor Coleridge,* Constable, 1956

Richard Holmes, *Coleridge: Early Visions,* Flamingo, 1989

Mary Moorman, *William Wordsworth: A Biography of the Early Years 1770–1803,* OUP, 1969

Ernest de Selincourt, *The Early Letters of William and Dorothy Wordsworth,* OUP, 1935

Dorothy Wordsworth, *Journals,* ed. Mary Moorman, OUP, 1971

CRITICISM

Patrick Campbell, *Wordsworth and Coleridge: 'Lyrical Ballads',* Palgrave Macmillan, 1991
    Surveys critical approaches to *Lyrical Ballads,* especially the most recent. *The Rime of the Ancyent Marinere,* 'Tintern Abbey', 'The Thorn' and 'The Idiot Boy' receive individual treatment. Considers the unity of the collection

FURTHER READING

Cynthia Chase, *Romanticism*, Longman, 1993
   Essays exemplifying recent feminist, deconstructive, and new historicist writing, including
   Paul de Man, Mary Jacobus, Marjorie Levinson and Jerome Christensen

S. Curran, *Poetic Form and British Romanticism*, OUP, 1986
   Looks at how the Romantics adapted traditional poetic forms to their own purposes

Aidan Day, *The New Critical Idiom: Romanticism*, Routledge, 1996
   Examines the nature of Romanticism and debates on the subject, with much attention given to Blake,
   Wordsworth, Coleridge, Keats and Shelley

Jennifer Ford, *Coleridge on Dreaming: Romanticism, Dreams and the Medical Imagination*,
CUP, 1998
   Looks at Coleridge's responses to his dreams and their influence on his poetry

Peter J. Kitson (ed.), *Coleridge, Keats and Shelley: New Casebooks*, Palgrave Macmillan, 1996
   Surveys modern critical approaches to these poets and how they are developing

J. Lowes, *The Road to Xanadu*, Constable, 1927; new edn 1951
   The story of the genesis of *The Rime of the Ancyent Marinere* and 'Kubla Khan'

R. Mayo, 'The contemporaneity of the *Lyrical Ballads*', *PMLA* LXIX, 1954, pp. 486–522
   Important article arguing that *Lyrical Ballads* was not a radical departure in terms of subject matter
   and style

Martin McQuillian, *Routledge Critical Thinkers: Paul De Man*, 2001
   Surveys the critical work of deconstructionist Paul De Man

Lucy Newlyn (ed.) *The Cambridge Companion to Coleridge*, 2002
   A comprehensive study, with essays on *The Rime of the Ancyent Marinere*, *Christabel* and
   Biographia Literaria

— *Coleridge, Wordsworth and the Language of Allusion*, OUP, 2001
   Explores the radical differences, theoretical and imaginative, between Wordsworth and Coleridge,
   and the creative effects of their misunderstandings

Nicola Trott and Seamus Perry (eds), *1800: The New Lyrical Ballads*, Palgrave Macmillan, 2001
   Essays in cultural history and biographical reconstruction, as well as analyses of the poems and their
   critics

John Williams, *Critical Issues: William Wordsworth*, Palgrave Macmillan, 2002
  Looks at the evolution of Wordsworth's work, and at the development of his reputation, giving a critical overview from the end of the eighteenth century to modern times

AUGUSTAN AND ROMANTIC POETRY

Elizabeth Barrett Browning, *Sonnets from the Portuguese*, 1850

William Blake, *Songs of Innocence and of Experience,* 1794

John Clare, *The Rural Muse*, 1835

William Cowper, *Olney Hymns*, 1779
— *The Task*, 1785

John Dryden, *Amphitryon*, 1690

Oliver Goldsmith, *The Deserted Village*, 1770

Thomas Gray, *Selected Poems*, Bloomsbury, 1997

John Keats, *Poems*, 1817
— *Endymion*, 1818
— *Poetical Works*, 1834

Alexander Pope, *Selected Poetry*, Oxford World Classics, 1998

Percy Bysshe Shelley, *Posthumous Poems*, 1824 (see also *Percy Bysshe Shelley* [Everyman], 1998)

Alfred, Lord Tennyson, *Poems, Chiefly Lyrical*, 1830

ROMANTIC NOVELS

Ann Radcliffe, *The Italian*, 1797

Walter Scott, *The Heart of Midlothian*, 1818
— *Rob Roy*, 1818
— *Ivanhoe*, 1819

Mary Shelley, *Frankenstein*, 1818

allegory a story or a situation with two different levels, where the story on the surface is used to symbolise a deeper meaning underneath. This secondary meaning is often a spiritual or moral one whose values are represented by specific figures, characters or events in the **narrative**

alliteration the repetition of the same consonant or a sequence of vowels in a stretch of language, most often at the beginnings of words or on stressed syllables

allusion a passing reference in a work of literature to something outside the text; may include other works of literature, myth, historical facts or biographical detail

anapaestic of metre, having two unstressed syllables followed by one stressed

ballad a traditional form of poetry telling a story, often tragic, usually in four-line stanzas, in iambic metre, the first and third lines having four stresses, the second and fourth having three, rhyming *abcb*

blank verse unrhymed **iambic pentameter**

conceit an extended or elaborate concept that forges an unexpected connection between two apparently dissimilar things

couplet a pair of rhymed lines of any metre

diction an author's word choice

end-stopped of a line of verse the end of which coincides with the end of a sentence or clause

enjambment in poetry, when a sentence runs on from one line to the next, and even from one stanza to the next

feminine rhyme rhyming of stressed penultimate syllables, each followed by an unstressed syllable

framed narrative a narrative containing another narrative within itself, often with both being in the words of first-person narrators

gothic describing a poem or story featuring castles, dungeons, gloomy mansions, death and decay, etc.

gothic romance as above but specifically relating to a story, usually focusing on an individual

iambic pentameter a line of poetry consisting of five iambic feet (iambic consisting of a weak syllable followed by a strong one)

imagery descriptive language which uses images to make actions, objects and characters more vivid in the reader's mind. **Metaphors** and **similes** are examples of imagery

irony the humorous or sarcastic use of words to imply the opposite of what they normally mean; incongruity between what might be expected and what actually happens; the ill-timed arrival of an event that had been hoped for

metaphor a figure of speech in which a word or phrase is applied to an object, a character or an action which does not literally belong to it, in order to imply a resemblance and create an unusual or striking image in the reader's mind

metre the rhythmic arrangement of syllables in poetic verse

metrical foot a group of two or more syllables in which one of the syllables has the major stress. The basic unit of poetic rhythm

narrative a story, tale or any recital of events, and the manner in which it is told. First person narratives ('I') are told from the character's perspective and usually require the reader to judge carefully what is being said; second person narratives ('you') suggest the reader is part of the story; in third person narratives ('he', 'she', 'they') the narrator may be intrusive (continually commenting on the story), impersonal, or omniscient. More than one style of narrative may be used in a text

narrator the voice telling the story or relating a sequence of events

ode a serious lyric poem celebrating a particular event or subject

pantheism a belief system, to which Coleridge particularly subscribed, which holds that the natural world is a material reflection of God

parable story, especially in the Bible, whose purpose is to teach a moral lesson

parody an imitation of a work of literature or a literary style designed to ridicule the original

persona(e) the use of an imagined character as the voice or speaker of a poem

personification the treatment or description of an object or an idea as human, with human attributes and feelings

quadrameter line of verse with four metrical feet

quatrain four-lined **stanza**

rhetoric the art of speaking (and writing) effectively so as to persuade an audience

Romantics followers of a movement in the arts which reacted to the rationalist Age of Enlightenment and the Industrial Revolution, emphasising individualism, the power of nature, social equality and the irrational

satire a type of literature in which folly, evil or topical issues are held up to scorn through ridicule, irony or exaggeration

simile a figure of speech which compares two things using the words 'like' or 'as'

LITERARY TERMS

sonnet a poem of fourteen lines, usually in two parts, an octet and a sextet, with a definite rhyme scheme, normally in **iambic pentameter**

stanza in a poem when lines of verse are grouped together into units; these units are called stanzas. They usually follow a pattern with a fixed number of lines and a set number of **metrical feet** within each line

symbolism investing material objects with abstract powers and meanings greater than their own; allowing a complex idea to be represented by a single object

syntax the grammatical way in which words combine to create meaning

tetrameter metre consisting of four feet per line

unreliable narrator narrator who gives a biased or imperfect account

AUTHOR OF THESE NOTES

Steve Eddy graduated from the University of Warwick with an honours degree in English and American Literature. He has taught English at secondary level and is the author of numerous English text books and GCSE and A Level literature study guides. These include guides to several Shakespeare plays, Thomas Hardy, John Steinbeck and Mildred Taylor, and YNA titles on William Golding's *The Spire*, Philip Larkin's *High Windows* and *The Brontës: Selected Poems*. He has also published a number of books on mythology.

GCSE

Maya Angelou
I Know Why the Caged Bird Sings

Jane Austen
Pride and Prejudice

Alan Ayckbourn
Absent Friends

Elizabeth Barrett Browning
Selected Poems

Robert Bolt
A Man for All Seasons

Harold Brighouse
Hobson's Choice

Charlotte Brontë
Jane Eyre

Emily Brontë
Wuthering Heights

Brian Clark
Whose Life is it Anyway?

Robert Cormier
Heroes

Shelagh Delaney
A Taste of Honey

Charles Dickens
David Copperfield
Great Expectations
Hard Times
Oliver Twist
Selected Stories

Roddy Doyle
Paddy Clarke Ha Ha Ha

George Eliot
The Mill on the Floss
Silas Marner

Anne Frank
The Diary of a Young Girl

William Golding
Lord of the Flies

Oliver Goldsmith
She Stoops to Conquer

Willis Hall
The Long and the Short and the Tall

Thomas Hardy
Far from the Madding Crowd
The Mayor of Casterbridge
Tess of the d'Urbervilles
The Withered Arm and other Wessex Tales

L. P. Hartley
The Go-Between

Seamus Heaney
Selected Poems

Susan Hill
I'm the King of the Castle

Barry Hines
A Kestrel for a Knave

Louise Lawrence
Children of the Dust

Harper Lee
To Kill a Mockingbird

Laurie Lee
Cider with Rosie

Arthur Miller
The Crucible
A View from the Bridge

Robert O'Brien
Z for Zachariah

Frank O'Connor
My Oedipus Complex and Other Stories

George Orwell
Animal Farm

J. B. Priestley
An Inspector Calls
When We Are Married

Willy Russell
Educating Rita
Our Day Out

J. D. Salinger
The Catcher in the Rye

William Shakespeare
Henry IV Part I
Henry V
Julius Caesar
Macbeth
The Merchant of Venice
A Midsummer Night's Dream
Much Ado About Nothing
Romeo and Juliet
The Tempest
Twelfth Night

George Bernard Shaw
Pygmalion

Mary Shelley
Frankenstein

R. C. Sherriff
Journey's End

Rukshana Smith
Salt on the Snow

John Steinbeck
Of Mice and Men

Robert Louis Stevenson
Dr Jekyll and Mr Hyde

Jonathan Swift
Gulliver's Travels

Robert Swindells
Daz 4 Zoe

Mildred D. Taylor
Roll of Thunder, Hear My Cry

Mark Twain
Huckleberry Finn

James Watson
Talking in Whispers

Edith Wharton
Ethan Frome

William Wordsworth
Selected Poems

A Choice of Poets

Mystery Stories of the Nineteenth Century including The Signalman

Nineteenth Century Short Stories

Poetry of the First World War

Six Women Poets

For the AQA Anthology:
Duffy and Armitage & Pre-1914 Poetry

Heaney and Clarke & Pre-1914 Poetry

Poems from Different Cultures

Key Stage 3

William Shakespeare
Much Ado About Nothing
Richard III
The Tempest

Margaret Atwood
Cat's Eye
The Handmaid's Tale

Jane Austen
Emma
Mansfield Park
Persuasion
Pride and Prejudice
Sense and Sensibility

Pat Barker
Regeneration

William Blake
Songs of Innocence and of Experience

The Brontës
Selected Poems

Charlotte Brontë
Jane Eyre
Villette

Emily Brontë
Wuthering Heights

Angela Carter
The Bloody Chamber
Nights at the Circus
Wise Children

Geoffrey Chaucer
The Franklin's Prologue and Tale
The Merchant's Prologue and Tale
The Miller's Prologue and Tale
The Pardoner's Tale
The Prologue to the Canterbury Tales
The Wife of Bath's Prologue and Tale

Caryl Churchill
Top Girls

John Clare
Selected Poems

Joseph Conrad
Heart of Darkness

Charles Dickens
Bleak House
Great Expectations
Hard Times

John Donne
Selected Poems

Carol Ann Duffy
Selected Poems
The World's Wife

George Eliot
Middlemarch
The Mill on the Floss

T. S. Eliot
Selected Poems
The Waste Land

Sebastian Faulks
Birdsong

F. Scott Fitzgerald
The Great Gatsby

John Ford
'Tis Pity She's a Whore

John Fowles
The French Lieutenant's Woman

Michael Frayn
Spies

Charles Frazier
Cold Mountain

Brian Friel
Making History
Translations

William Golding
The Spire

Thomas Hardy
Jude the Obscure
The Mayor of Casterbridge
The Return of the Native
Selected Poems
Tess of the d'Urbervilles

Nathaniel Hawthorne
The Scarlet Letter

Homer
The Iliad
The Odyssey

Khaled Hosseini
The Kite Runner

Aldous Huxley
Brave New World

Henrik Ibsen
A Doll's House

James Joyce
Dubliners

John Keats
Selected Poems

Philip Larkin
High Windows
The Whitsun Weddings and Selected Poems

Ian McEwan
Atonement

Christopher Marlowe
Doctor Faustus
Edward II

Arthur Miller
All My Sons
Death of a Salesman

John Milton
Paradise Lost Books I and II

George Orwell
Nineteen Eighty-Four

Sylvia Plath
Selected Poems

William Shakespeare
Antony and Cleopatra
As You Like It
Hamlet
Henry IV Part I
King Lear
Macbeth
Measure for Measure
The Merchant of Venice
A Midsummer Night's Dream
Much Ado About Nothing
Othello
Richard II
Richard III
Romeo and Juliet
The Taming of the Shrew
The Tempest
Twelfth Night
The Winter's Tale

Mary Shelley
Frankenstein

Richard Brinsley Sheridan
The School for Scandal

Bram Stoker
Dracula

Alfred Tennyson
Selected Poems

Virgil
The Aeneid

Alice Walker
The Color Purple

John Webster
The Duchess of Malfi
The White Devil

Oscar Wilde
The Importance of Being Earnest
The Picture of Dorian Gray
A Woman of No Importance

Tennessee Williams
Cat on a Hot Tin Roof
The Glass Menagerie
A Streetcar Named Desire

Jeanette Winterson
Oranges Are Not the Only Fruit

Virginia Woolf
To the Lighthouse

William Wordsworth
The Prelude and Selected Poems

Wordsworth and Coleridge
Lyrical Ballads

Poetry of the First World War